CLIVE

ULTIMATE
SPORTS HEROES

FORMULA 1
GREATEST MOMENTS

ULTIMATE RACES,
CARS AND GLORY

DINO

First published in the UK in 2025 by Dino Books,
an imprint of Bonnier Books UK,
5th Floor, HYLO, 105 Bunhill Row,
London, EC1Y 8LZ
www.bonnierbooks.co.uk

Copyright © 2025 Studio Press

All rights reserved. No part of this publication may be reproduced or transmitted in any form or by any means, electronic, or mechanical, including photocopying, recording, or by any information storage and retrieval system, without permission in writing from the publisher.

1 3 5 7 9 10 8 6 4 2

978 1 78946 908 0

Written by Clive Gifford
Cover illustrated by Dan Leydon
Edited by Frankie Jones
Designed by Maddox Philpot
Production by Natalie Tang

FSC www.fsc.org — MIX Paper | Supporting responsible forestry — FSC® C018072

The authorised representative in the EEA is Bonnier Books UK (Ireland) Limited.
Registered office address: Floor 3, Block 3, Miesian Plaza
50–58 Baggot Street Lower,
Dublin 2, D02 Y754, Ireland.
compliance@bonnierbooks.ie

The views in this book are the author's own and the copyright, trademarks and names are that of their respective owners and are not intended to suggest endorsement, agreement, affiliation or otherwise of any kind.

This book is unofficial and unauthorised and is not endorsed by or affiliated with Formula 1.

All statistics are accurate to the first race of 2025.

A CIP catalogue record for this book is available from the British Library
Printed and bound in Great Britain by Clays Ltd, Elcograf S.p.A

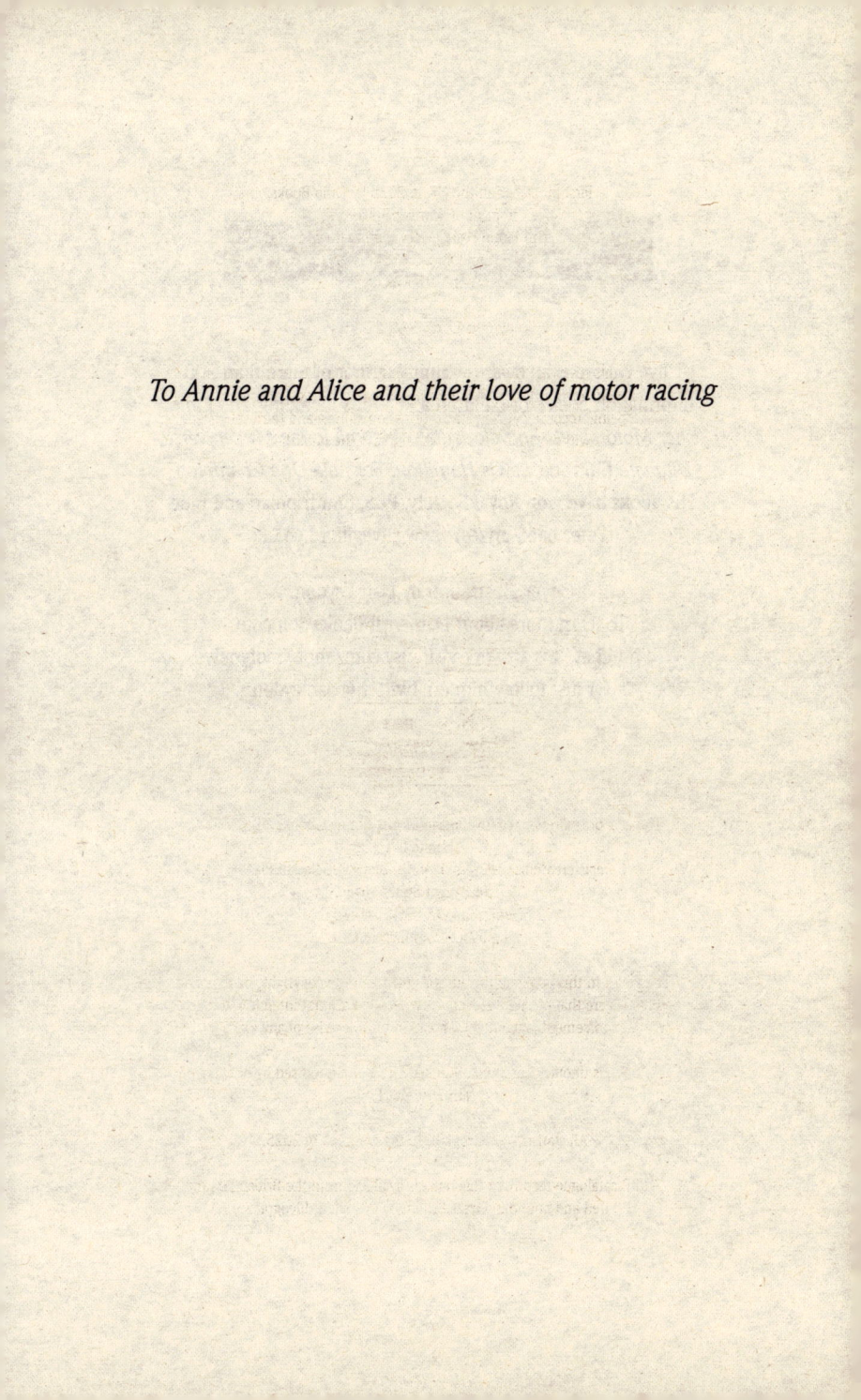

To Annie and Alice and their love of motor racing

ULTIMATE SPORTS HEROES

Clive Gifford is an award-winning author of more than 200 information books for children and adults including *The Kingfisher Motorsports Encyclopedia, Welcome to the Mysteryverse, Ultimate Cars* and *Lewis Hamilton: Formula One Champion.* His books have won Royal Society, PBS, Smithsonian and Blue Peter book prizes. www.clivegifford.co.uk

Cover illustration by Dan Leydon.
To learn more about Dan, visit danleydon.com
To purchase his artwork visit etsy.com/shop/footynews
Or just follow him on Twitter @danleydon

ACKNOWLEDGEMENTS

Many thanks to Russell McLean (one day we will do the 12-hour lawnmower race at Wisborough Green) and to Frankie Jones and Justin Lewis for making the writing and editing of this book such a joy. Many thanks also to the tireless staff of Trafford Libraries for putting up with all my research requests and the occasional overdue book (sorry!), to Rob at M&M Automotive for his help and to Steve Mersereau for his unceasing passion for all things F1.

Last but not least, to my mother, who despite not learning to drive was a mad keen fan of motorsport and could (and did) talk for hours about Lewis Hamilton's chances in the wet at Hockenheim and Monza.

AUTHOR'S NOTE

Formula 1 is the ultimate in motor racing. It's packed full of speed, action and drama. The world's top racing drivers roar round amazing tracks in tech-filled cars pushing themselves to the limit.

You really need out-of-this-world skill, nerve and fitness to race an F1 car. I once did a few laps in a Formula Two car (not quite as fast or packed with tech as an F1 machine) but still *FAST*. It was terrifying! The enormous power, the sudden changes of speed and the forces pushing and pulling your body were incredible. I was exhausted after just three laps. You have to marvel at F1 drivers racing for 70 laps or more at even higher speeds.

Every F1 race has its moments of tension and drama, every season its extraordinary heroes and amazing performances. Picking just one hundred from the sport is a tough task. If I haven't included all of your favourite F1 moments, sorry. There are just so many.

I've included moments of crazy luck (good and bad), record-breaking feats, amazing innovations, as well as the sport's dark and dangerous side, the cheats, crashes and controversies.

I hope you enjoy reading the book as much as I did, researching and writing it.

Clive Gifford

WHERE IT ALL BEGAN

13 May 1950. King George VI of Britain watched on as 21 Formula 1 cars revved their engines. The British Grand Prix was about to begin. A big crowd of 150,000 racing fans were lined up all round the Silverstone race circuit.

It was a historic moment. It was the first ever race of Formula 1's World Championship of Drivers. The people who ran motorsport had been discussing a world championship since the 1930s. It had finally arrived.

Teams could enter more than two cars for the race. Alfa Romeo sent four. And all four qualified brilliantly, filling the four-car front row of the starting grid. In fifth place was a member of the Thai royal family, Prince Bira. He was driving a Maserati.

The other 17 cars were no match for the four Alfa Romeos. Although Juan Fangio's Alfa had to retire on the sixty-second lap, the other three Alfas took all three podium places. Giuseppe 'Nino' Farina crossed the finish line first, to win the first ever World Championship race.

The World Championship that year only consisted of seven races. Alfa didn't send their cars to America to compete in the Indy 500 race. But it didn't matter. Farina won two of the remaining five races – the Swiss Grand Prix and the Italian Grand Prix – to be crowned F1's first ever world champion.

EMILIO GIUSEPPE 'NINO' FARINA	
Born	1906, Turin, Italy
F1 Career	1950–56
Total races	35
F1 wins	5

WONDER IN THE WET

Max Verstappen rolled his Red Bull RB20 car into P17 on the starting grid. Having won more than 60 grand prix titles, seventeenth was not a place he usually found himself.

It was the start of the 2024 São Paulo Grand Prix in Brazil. Max had had a poor qualifying session plus a grid penalty for changing his car's engine. That's why he was so far back. To make things worse, his main rival for the 2024 World Drivers' title, Lando Norris, was on P1 – pole position – right at the front.

Lights off. Race on!

The Interlagos track was wet as the rain fell, but that didn't hold Max back. Driving masterfully, he moved up seven places… just on the opening lap. Racing rival Oscar Piastri couldn't believe what he saw. 'He seemed to be pretty much the only one that could overtake,' the young Australian said.

As others faltered, Verstappen drove without making a mistake. He reeled off five consecutive fastest laps of the race as he passed more and more cars. His very fastest lap was over a second quicker than any other driver could manage. Max was flying.

On lap 43, he swept by Esteban Ocon to take the lead and never gave it up. Verstappen crossed the line more than nineteen seconds ahead of his nearest rival. It was a drive praised by current and former F1 legends alike as one of the best drives ever seen. It helped him on his way to his fourth world title in a row.

MAX EMILIAN VERSTAPPEN	
Born	1997, Hasselt, Belgium
F1 Career	2015–
Total races	210
F1 wins	63

AGE NO BARRIER

Born before the start of the twentieth century, Louis Chiron began his racing career in 1923, long before there was a Formula 1 World Championship. He won grands prix all over Europe including the Italian GP (1928), the German GP (1929), and the French Grand Prix five times (1931, 1934, 1937, 1947, 1949). He was the first driver from Monaco to win his home grand prix in 1931.

Chiron was 50 years old when the F1 World Championship began in 1950. Some thought he was too old to take part, but he was excited by the challenge. He managed to finish third at the 1950 Monaco Grand Prix.

Five years later, in front of a cheering home crowd, Chiron was still in F1 and starting the 1955 Monaco GP. He began in lowly nineteenth place, but guided his Lancia D50 expertly around the circuit's tight and treacherous turns. His reward was an amazing sixth place finish, ahead of F1 greats like Juan Fangio and Stirling Moss.

At 55 years, nine months and 19 days old, Chiron was – and remains – the oldest driver ever to complete an F1 race. Turn 13 of the Monte Carlo race circuit used for the Monaco Grand Prix is named Chiron in his honour.

LOUIS ALEXANDRE CHIRON	
Born	1899, Monte Carlo, Monaco
F1 Career	1950–51, 1953, 1955–56, 1958
Total races	19
F1 wins	0

ON TOP OF THE WORLD

It was all on the line for the last race of the 1958 season. British driver Mike Hawthorn had only won one grand prix that year, in France, but his pace and the reliability of his Ferrari meant he had also finished second five times. He went into the final race eight points ahead of Stirling Moss in the Drivers' Championship.

It was the first ever Moroccan Grand Prix, held in Casablanca, and Moss had to win and hope his British rival finished well down the field. But Hawthorn was determined to win the championship. In 1953, he had been the first British driver to win an F1 World Championship race when he beat the great Juan Fangio in an epic battle at the French Grand Prix.

Moss blasted into the lead at the Morocco Grand Prix, but Hawthorn, who always wore a bow tie when racing, kept pace. He drove carefully as a crash or his car breaking down would shatter his world title dreams.

Hawthorn crossed the finish line after 53 gruelling laps in second place in the race. He had done it! He had won the championship – the first British driver to do so. Hours later, he announced his retirement from racing. He had achieved what he most wanted to do: become champion of the world.

JOHN MICHAEL HAWTHORN	
Born	1929, Doncaster, England
F1 Career	1952–58
Total races	47
F1 wins	3

HAMILTON ARRIVES IN STYLE

The last race of the 2008 season saw all eyes on Lewis Hamilton. He only needed to finish fifth, or better, to defeat Ferrari's Felipe Massa and be crowned World Champion. And all during only his second season in F1.

Hamilton guided his McLaren car carefully around the rapid Interlagos circuit in Brazil. He powered down the Reta Oposta straight at 320 km/h but kept out of trouble. There were only two laps to go and he was fifth. But heavy rain had just started falling, making the track wet and slippery. It was too late to pit for new tyres, and Hamilton had to wrestle with his car as it slipped and slid all over the track.

Sebastian Vettel took advantage and overtook Hamilton. Disaster! With Massa leading the race, the chance of World Championship glory appeared to have gone. Certainly, the Ferrari team thought so. They started celebrating wildly in the pit lane when Massa crossed the line to win the race.

Thirty-eight seconds behind Massa on the track, though, there was some truly incredible drama unfolding. Hamilton drove with laser precision, noting Vettel taking fourth place and Timo Glock now in fifth. Approaching the last corner of the last lap of the race, Hamilton swooped past Glock. He regained fifth place just moments before speeding across the finish line. The McLaren team went crazy. Lewis Hamilton was World Champion!

Hamilton became Britain's ninth World Champion and the first Black driver to grab the ultimate prize. At just 23 years old, he was also the youngest World Champion. It was the start of a stellar career.

LEWIS CARL DAVIDSON HAMILTON	
Born	1985, Stevenage, England
F1 Career	2007–
Total races	357
F1 wins	105

FIRST WIN

The 2024 Hungarian Grand Prix was a memorable day out for one young Australian racing driver. Oscar Piastri had spent the previous season understudying Lando Norris at McLaren. Piastri had some great performances that season including his first podium finish (finishing first, second or third) at the 2023 Japanese Grand Prix. The FIA, which runs world motorsport, awarded him the title of Rookie of the Year.

He started the 2024 race in Hungary second on the grid with his teammate beside him. After four fourth place finishes and two second places this season, Piastri wanted more. He was hungry for his first F1 win.

As the five red lights switched off to start the race, Piastri tore away. Gunning his McLaren down the straight, he held the inside line to the first bend. Despite immense pressure from Norris, plus Max Verstappen swooping round the outside, Piastri held the first bend and raced away in first place.

Lap after lap saw him hold his lead until the McLaren cars were called into the pits for fresh tyres. The pit stops put Norris into the lead but the team insisted the two cars swapped places. Piastri won the race by two seconds, becoming only the fifth Australian driver to win a grand prix. He celebrated on the podium with Norris and Lewis Hamilton who was making his two hundredth podium appearance. Four races later, at the Azerbaijan Grand Prix, he notched his second F1 win.

OSCAR JACK PIASTRI	
Born	2001, Melbourne, Australia
F1 Career	2023–
Total races	47
F1 wins	2

WRONG BOX

Even the most experienced F1 drivers make mistakes. Jenson Button had been world champion in 2009 and had raced in Formula 1 for 11 years when he made a classic gaff at the 2011 Chinese Grand Prix. Button was leading the race in his McLaren when he headed into the pits.

'I was looking down at the steering wheel to adjust a switch,' he said in an after-race interview. 'And when I looked up, I thought I was in my pit box.'

It was only when he saw all the Red Bull team mechanics waving frantically at him that he realised… He'd driven into the wrong team pits! What's more, Red Bull driver Sebastian Vettel was close behind. He wanted to pit but couldn't, as there was a McLaren in his way.

A red-faced Jenson moved to his own team pits, rejoined the race and finished in fourth place. Vettel, who saw the funny side afterwards, finished second.

JENSON ALEXANDER LYONS BUTTON	
Born	1980, Frome, England
F1 Career	2000–2017
Total races	309
F1 wins	15

SURVIVING A FIREBALL

Formula 1 has always been a very dangerous sport but advances in technology have made it much safer than in the past. These include devices like the Halo, a collection of metal bars around the cockpit which protect the driver's head. Drivers also wear fire-resistant racing suits, which can withstand scorching temperatures of up to 800°C.

Shocking events at the 2020 Bahrain Grand Prix demonstrated how these advances in safety can save lives.

After ten years in the sport, Romain Grosjean was retiring at the end of the 2020 season. There were just three races to go when he powered his Haas car off the start line in Bahrain. He hadn't even completed the first lap when his car collided with Daniil Kvyat's vehicle and flew off at high speed into a solid steel safety barrier. His car split in two and blew up into a colossal fireball.

Astonishingly, 28 seconds later, Grosjean managed to limp away from the wreckage, helped by race stewards. His car, helmet and race clothing had saved his life. He suffered a sprained ankle, and needed surgery on burns to his hands, but was otherwise okay.

Showing no ill signs from his crash, Grosjean moved from Formula 1 to IndyCar racing in North America. There, he has reached the podium six times, to go with his ten podiums in F1.

ROMAIN DAVID JEREMIE GROSJEAN	
Born	1986, Geneva, Switzerland
F1 Career	2009, 2012–2020
Total races	181
F1 wins	0

PUSHING THE LIMIT

Roaring around the Sebring circuit in his Cooper, Australian driver Jack Brabham was sitting pretty. He was leading the 1959 US Grand Prix and only needed fourth place or better to win his first F1 World Championship.

His teammate Bruce McLaren was in second, and the pair had such a large lead over everyone else that Brabham was able to slow down and nurse his car to the end of the race.

All seemed well until there were just two corners to go on the last lap. The Climax engine in Brabham's car began spluttering. The car had run out of fuel! Meanwhile, Bruce McLaren passed his teammate to take the chequered flag, followed by Maurice Trintignant in second place.

Brabham's car had come to a standstill more than 300 metres short of the finish line. Its driver leapt out of the car, and already exhausted from a long race, he began pushing his vehicle towards the finish line. As he did so, Tony Brooks in his Ferrari passed to take third place. Brabham kept pushing. Finally, he shoved the car over the line to take fourth place. The World Championship was his. Phew!

JOHN ARTHUR 'JACK' BRABHAM	
Born	1926, Hurstville, Australia
F1 Career	1955–70
Total races	128
F1 wins	14

UNLUCKY AMON

Chris Amon learned to race by borrowing old cars in his native New Zealand and speeding around his parents' farm. He was considered a great talent in Formula 1 and won many races in other competitions, but seemed to suffer from really bad luck... right from his very first race.

Amon debuted at the 1963 Monaco Grand Prix but when the car of his teammate, Maurice Trintignant, developed problems, the senior driver got to use the rookie's car. There was no spare car, so Amon had to watch the race as a spectator.

When he moved to the newly-formed McLaren team in 1965, the team didn't have a car for him. So, Amon went off to race sports cars for much of the season.

And even when he *did* get to take part in grand prix racing, his cars seemed dogged with mechanical problems.

He had to retire from 45 F1 races.

After so many retirements in previous races, Amon grabbed his chance at the 1968 Spanish Grand Prix. Now driving for Ferrari, he was lightning fast in qualifying and finished half a second ahead of his rivals. It was his first pole position in F1.

Things looked good during the Spanish GP as he built a commanding lead. He was more than a minute ahead of second-placed Graham Hill. Then, disaster struck on the fifty-seventh lap. His Ferrari's fuel pump broke and the car ground to a halt. He had to walk all the way back to the pits as Hill sped past. Amon would get close again in subsequent races, but he would never win a Formula 1 race.

CHRISTOPHER ARTHUR AMON	
Born	1943, Bulls, New Zealand
F1 Career	1963–76
Total races	108
F1 wins	0

SLOW AND NO GO

Ernst Loof made his F1 debut in 1953 at the German Grand Prix in a Veritas Meteor, a car he had designed himself. As the race began, the roar of the engines reached fever pitch. Loof hit the accelerator and attempted to power off the line. His car surged forward then stopped suddenly. It had a broken fuel pump. Loof's race was over and he never took part in F1 again.

He does hold the record for the shortest distance raced as a Formula 1 driver – a grand total of two metres.

Sixteen years later, another unwanted F1 record was set, this time by Canadian driver, Al Pease. In his F1 race, the 1967 Canadian Grand Prix, he was lapped 43 times by the eventual winner, Jack Brabham. Pease only completed 47 of the scheduled 90 laps before the race was over.

Two years later at the same track, Pease tried again. Not only was he as slow as before, but he was getting in the way of far faster cars. Pease was on his twenty-second lap (the race leaders were on their forty-first) when the officials had had enough. They waved a black flag at him which meant he was disqualified from the race for driving too slowly – the only F1 participant to ever suffer such a fate.

ERNST LOOF	
Born	1907, Neindorf, Germany
F1 Career	1953
Total races	1
F1 wins	0

AMAZING MATCHING TIMES

The European Grand Prix, held at the Jerez circuit in Spain, was the last race of the 1997 F1 season. The Canadian driver, Jacques Villeneuve set a scorching pace in qualifying. His time around the track drew gasps from the crowd: 1 minute, 21.072 seconds. Pole position was his, surely.

Fourteen minutes later, the German great, Michael Schumacher took his own qualifying hot lap. Pushing his Ferrari F310B to the limit, Schumacher sped expertly round the track. His time flashed up on the screen – 1 minute, 21.072 seconds – the exact same time as Villeneuve's.

A few minutes later, Heinz-Harald Frentzen in his Williams-Renault car matched the others. It's the only time in history there have been three drivers tied at the top of qualifying. There could only be one car on pole, though, and the officials gave it to Villeneuve, because he had been the first to set the time.

FORMULA 1 GREATEST MOMENTS

FUTURE FEMALE STARS

The F1 Academy was set up by Formula 1 in 2023 to help up-and-coming female racing talent. It's hoped that competitions like this will lead to competitive female drivers starring in grand prix in the future.

Drivers between the ages of 16 and 25 compete in 21 F1 Academy races in Europe and the United States. The champion in 2023, Marta García, received a place in the Formula Regional European Championship, a step closer to the dream of racing in Formula 1.

García had been a karting star in her teens. The Spanish driver had won the highly prized FIA Karting Academy Trophy in 2015, won four years earlier by F1 star Charles Leclerc.

Marta García stormed through the 2023 F1 Academy season, winning seven races and finishing either second or third a further five times that season. She won the championship with two races to go. Outstanding!

MARTA GARCÍA LÓPEZ	
Born	2000, Dénia, Spain
F1 Academy career	2023
Total races	23
F1 Academy wins	7

MARVELLOUS MURRAY

For more than 50 years, F1 fans often watched races on TV to the sounds of Murray Walker's voice.

Walker's first race commentary – the 1949 British Grand Prix – predated the World F1 Championship by a year, and yet he was still commentating in 2001. Walker reported on F1 races with a passion. His voice often rose in pitch and volume as the cars roared by and the race action unfolded. He formed great double acts with retired racing drivers such as James Hunt and Jonathan Palmer.

Walker did lots of research before each race and spoke behind the scenes with team bosses and drivers. But, sometimes, in the heat of commentating on a fast-moving race, he might get his thoughts and words in a muddle with, often, hilarious results.

Walker's errors became known as Murrayisms and were enjoyed by many race fans:

> 'Unless I am mistaken… And I am VERY MUCH mistaken…'

> 'There is nothing wrong with the car, apart from that it is on fire.'

> 'The lead car is totally unique, apart from the car behind it, which is identical.'

> 'Jean Alesi is fourth and fifth.'

> 'I'm ready to stop my start watch.'

A few fans found him irritating but most enjoyed his love of Formula 1. As the ex-F1 driver, David Coulthard said of him, 'He made even the most boring race sound interesting.'

THE OUT OF FUEL FINISH

One of the strangest finishes in F1 history took place at the 1985 San Marino Grand Prix. With just four laps to go, Ayrton Senna in his Lotus was cruising to victory. But following lap after lap of intense racing, fuel consumption had been high. Suddenly, Senna slowed…

…he'd run out of fuel!

Stefan Johansson was only in his second F1 race for Ferrari. He couldn't believe his good luck. He passed Senna and victory was surely his until…

…he ran out of fuel as well!

Alain Prost passed Johansson's slowing car to take a surprise win. Elio de Angelis finished second and it looked like Thierry Boutsen would come third.

However, Boutsen's car also ran out of fuel just short of the finish line. Boutsen smartly hopped out of the cockpit and pushed his Arrows-BMW car over the line to gain a podium place by just three seconds. Phew!

There was, however, a sting in the tail. When the race officials examined the cars, they found Alain Prost's McLaren was two kilogrammes below the minimum weight. He was disqualified, making de Angelis the winner and bumping Boutsen up to second place.

WILLIAMS WINS

In 1977, after failing to find success with his previous race team, Frank Williams joined forces with the young car designer, Patrick Head. They formed a team called Williams Racing. By 1980, the team had the perfect match of driver – the no-nonsense Australian, Alan Jones – and a powerful brute of a car, the Williams FW07B, designed by Head.

The 1980 season got off to a flying start at the Argentine Grand Prix. Despite coming off the track twice and needing a pit stop to clear grass out of his car's radiator, Jones won. Brilliant! Later in the season, he became the first Australian ever to win the Australian Grand Prix. He also triumphed at the French and British Grand Prix.

Racing in his lucky red underpants, Jones and the car were rapid and reliable. He made the podium in

10 out of the 14 championship races, winning five of them. By the time of the last-but-one race, the Canadian Grand Prix, Jones and the team knew a win would give him the title. He fended off key rival Nelson Piquet masterfully and crossed the line first.

Jones became Australia's second ever World Champion after Jack Brabham (see p. 24). Williams also won their first ever Constructors' Championship, and the team would go on to win another eight titles in the 1980s and 1990s as one of the dominant forces in F1.

ALAN JONES	
Born	1946, Melbourne, Australia
F1 career	1975–86
Total races	117
F1 wins	12

POLE POSITION

Robert Kubica became F1's first ever driver from Poland when he signed for the BMW Sauber team in 2006. But the following year, at the Canadian Grand Prix, he suffered a horrific crash.

After a tussle with Jarno Trulli, Kubica's car struggled with a broken front wing and its nose lifted into the air. This meant he was unable to steer or brake and he crashed into a solid concrete wall at over 300 kilometres per hour. CRUNCH!

The car bounced across the track, flipping over and then smashing into the safety barriers on the other side. The car was wrecked and spectators feared the worst as the young Pole was rushed to hospital. But he was largely uninjured and his first words to his race team at his bedside were, 'Can I race at Indianapolis next weekend?'

Returning to Montreal for the same race the following year, Kubica must have felt nerves. But he certainly didn't show them as he blasted round the track in qualifying to start the race in second place beside Lewis Hamilton.

An incident in the pit lane between the cars of championship leaders Lewis Hamilton and Kimi Räikkönen saw both out of the race. After a pit stop himself, Kubica was back in second but swept past Nick Heidfeld, his BMW Sauber teammate, to take the lead.

Kubica controlled the rest of the race, winning by more than sixteen seconds to notch his first, and only, grand prix victory. It was also the first time since 1962 that a German constructor had won a World Championship F1 race.

ROBERT KUBICA	
Born	1984, Krakow, Poland
F1 career	2006–21
Total races	99
F1 wins	1

LAST TO FIRST... FOR A WHILE

Many drivers only get to take part in a single Formula 1 grand prix. German driver Markus Winkelhock was one of them, and he got his chance at the 2007 European GP race held at the fearsome Nürburgring circuit. Winkelhock qualified last, almost four-and-a-half seconds slower than Kimi Räikkönen on pole.

As the cars rounded the circuit on their formation lap before lining up to start, those on the track learnt that a very heavy downpour of rain was imminent.

'Box! Box! This lap!'

Winkelhock's team, Spyker, used his helmet radio to call him into the pits to change his tyres from dry to wet. It was an inspired decision as the rain began to fall just as the race started. All the other cars headed into the pits later in the first lap. The young German driver suddenly found himself leading the race. It was the first and only time a Spyker car ever led a grand prix.

Winkelhock's lead grew to a mammoth 35 seconds, but sadly, the fun didn't last. A hydraulics problem saw him forced to retire on the thirteenth lap. His race was over.

It was the only Formula 1 race he took part in, and he later described it as 'probably, the most exciting 15 minutes of my life.'

SPRINT TO SUCCESS

In 2021, Formula 1 introduced an extra race at some race weekends – sprint qualifying. This 100km-long race was held on the Saturday. The results of this race would decide the order of the starting grid for the main race, the Grand Prix, on the Sunday.

Fans at Silverstone were delighted when their home champion Lewis Hamilton seized sprint qualifying's first ever pole position. Alongside him, though, was his fierce rival Max Verstappen. And it was Verstappen who got the better start.

Roaring off the line, Verstappen took the lead and never lost it. Winning the seventeen-lap sprint not only gave him pole position for the main race but also added three points to his total in the Drivers' World Championship.

Although Verstappen lost out to Hamilton in the main race, he has since proven himself as the F1 sprint king. The Dutchman has won 11 sprint races whilst his nearest rivals, Oscar Piastri and Valtteri Bottas have only won two.

YOUNG GUN

English racing driver Oliver Bearman was a boy in a hurry. He was only twelve years old when he won the highly prized Kartmasters British Grand Prix in 2017. It wasn't long before he moved up from karting and began racing in Formula Four and Formula Three competitions.

Formula 1 teams took notice and he was given the chance to test F1 cars in practices. He impressed so much that both Ferrari and Haas made him a reserve driver for their 2024 F1 season.

In only the second F1 race of the season, though, Ferrari had a crisis. Their driver, Carlos Sainz had appendicitis and had been rushed to hospital. He certainly could not race. Bearman was called up as his replacement and was going to race in the Saudi Arabian Grand Prix.

Bearman showed no nerves as he qualified in eleventh place. This put him ahead of far more seasoned/experienced drivers including Daniel Ricciardo and Esteban Ocon. And he showed great pace and skill to move up the field during the race. He overtook Zhou Guanyu on the fourteenth lap, held off challenges from other cars and crossed the finish line in seventh. It was a brilliant debut drive and gained Ferrari six championship points.

At 18 years, 305 days old, Bearman was the youngest ever driver to score points on his F1 debut. 'He's done an incredible job,' purred his Ferrari teammate, Charles Leclerc. 'Everyone has noticed how talented he is.'

OLIVER JAMES BEARMAN	
Born	2005, Havering, England
F1 career	2024–
Total races	4
F1 wins	0

BLINK AND YOU'LL MISS IT

Formula 1 pit teams take pride in fast, slick pit stops. There may be twenty or more trained mechanics in each pit crew. These include jack men who lift the car up off the ground and tyre gunners who operate powerful wheel guns that loosen and tighten the bolts holding the wheels on.

All pit crews train really hard, practising every movement. They know that every saved fraction of a second gives their driver a greater chance of a higher finish during the race.

At the 2019 Brazilian Grand Prix, the Red Bull team were in amazing form. During the race, Max Verstappen in his RB15 car, roared into the pits for fresh tyres. The team replaced all four wheels in a pit stop lasting just 1.82 seconds.

This was a new record for the fastest pit stop during a grand prix. The crew won a trophy at the end of the season, but their real pride was helping Verstappen win the race.

THE FIRST LADY OF F1

Her brothers teased her and said a woman couldn't drive fast, but Maria Teresa de Filippis proved them wrong. As a 22-year-old, she won the first ever motor race she entered, a 10km cross-country sprint across Italy, despite driving a tiny, underpowered Fiat 500B.

De Filippis entered the 1954 Italian Sports Car Championship, and stunned spectators by finishing second overall. She certainly impressed famed Italian race team, Maserati who employed her as a works driver. She was now paid to drive, test and, occasionally, race fast cars. It was de Filippis's dream job.

In 1958, de Filippis got the chance she craved, entering that year's Belgian Grand Prix at the Spa-Francorchamps race track. Driving a Maserati 250F, she became the first woman to complete a

World Championship F1 race, finishing tenth. But at the next grand prix, in France, the race director refused to let a woman compete. Scandalous.

She took part in two more F1 World Championship races in 1958 – at Oporto in Portugal and Monza, Italy – but failed to finish either due to her car breaking down. It was especially galling at Monza as she was in fifth place, with just 13 of the 70 laps to go, when her car's engine cut out.

Her F1 career may have been short but de Filippis certainly made an impact. She later became Vice President of the Formula 1 Grand Prix Drivers Club.

MARIA TERESA DE FILIPPIS	
Born	1926, Naples, Italy
F1 career	1958–59
Total races	5
F1 wins	0

ICEMAN IN A HOT TUB

The Monaco Grand Prix is world famous for its spectacular setting. Part of the track runs along the principality's glitzy harbour lined with exotic luxury yachts – one of which was, in 2006, owned by the F1 driver, Kimi Räikkönen.

Räikkönen was known as a cool driver who never seemed to get flustered or emotional, hence his nickname of the Iceman. At the 2006 Monaco Grand Prix race, he qualified third in his McLaren MP4-21 and was driving well until disaster struck.

The heat shield that protects the car from the engine heat caught fire. It had blazed briefly earlier but the flames had been extinguished. This time, though, the fire burned through some of the car's electrical wiring. Räikkönen's race was over on lap 50.

After pulling the car off the track at the Poitier turn, everyone expected the Finnish driver to trudge back to his team in the pits. Räikkönen, though, had other plans.

Still in his race suit and helmet, he walked along the pavements of Monaco, entered the harbour and climbed aboard *One More Toy*, his own yacht. While the race continued, TV cameras showed pictures of him sitting in his yacht's hot tub, relaxing and watching the action!

Räikkönen left McLaren for Ferrari at the end of 2006. It proved a great move as he won the World Championship the following season. In 2023, the same ill-fated F1 car which he abandoned at Monaco sold at auction for a cool US$2.6 million.

PODIUM AT LAST

Martin Brundle is known for his F1 commentating and interviews on TV, but many years earlier, he was a daredevil hot rod racer. He then switched to Formula Three where he finished second overall to Ayrton Senna in the 1983 championship. Both drivers moved into Formula 1 the following year.

In his eighth grand prix, held in 1984 in the US city of Detroit, Brundle drove his Tyrrell 012 car to unexpected heights. He powered around the street circuit, closing in on leader Nelson Piquet. He ran out of laps to overtake the Brazilian driver so had to be content with second place. ...Or so he thought.

F1 officials later disqualified the Tyrrell team for the whole season for breaking the rules and making illegal modifications to their cars. Brundle was stripped of his podium place. Little did he know how long he would have to wait to get another.

By the time of the 1992 French Grand Prix, Brundle was a grizzled veteran of more than 90 F1 races. He now drove alongside an exciting young German driver called Michael Schumacher for the Benetton team. In the previous race in Canada, Brundle had overtaken his teammate and was cruising in second place. A podium finish was surely his... until his car broke down with gearbox trouble.

This time, at the French Grand Prix, Brundle would not be denied. He drove well and finished third, behind Riccardo Patrese and race winner, Nigel Mansell. It was Brundle's first podium finish after a gruelling career of 91 races – the longest wait for any F1 driver in history.

MARTIN JOHN BRUNDLE	
Born	1959, Kings Lynn, England
F1 career	1984–89, 1991–96
Total races	165
F1 wins	0

THE BLUFF THAT WORKED

In 1958, British racer Stirling Moss headed to South America with the two-man Walker team, comprising just two mechanics, Alf Francis and Timmy Wall. They were entering the Argentine Grand Prix.

The team's single car was a Cooper-Climax T43. It was underpowered and no match for the powerful Ferraris and Maseratis that Moss had to race against. The T43's wheels were held on by four long bolts. This meant that a pit stop for a change of tyres took minutes rather than seconds. But Moss and his mechanics had a grand plan…

From the start, Moss drove carefully, to look after his tyres and to stop them wearing out. Other teams lost precious seconds whenever they headed into the pits for a tyre change. Moss's rivals assumed he would be coming in for a tyre change too. Alf Francis stood by the track holding a tyre, pretending to wave Moss in, just to convince them further, but it was all a bluff. The team had no intention of stopping to change tyres. It was a risky move, too. Few drivers ever attempted a 313-kilometre long race on the one set of tyres.

As the remaining number of laps were counting down, Moss was still in the lead but the others were catching up. Almost all of his car tyres' rubber had worn away.

Moss drove brilliantly, battling with the lack of grip his tyres now provided. Luigi Musso in a Ferrari was closing in, but Moss held him off, and won the race by just 2.7 seconds. Musso was second, while Mike Hawthorn, also driving a Ferrari, was third. The Walker team's tactics were the talk of the race paddock for weeks afterwards!

STIRLING CRAUFURD MOSS	
Born	1929, London, England
F1 career	1951–61
Total races	67
F1 wins	16

A BIG BLOW OUT

Nigel Mansell was leading the 1986 Championship. He had won five races that season and topped the leaderboard, six points ahead of Alain Prost, who in turn was a point ahead of Nelson Piquet.

But with nine points for a race win, there was still a three-way-showdown for the title at the last race of the season, in Australia.

Mansell liked the circuit there which wound through the streets of Adelaide. He was tense but confident. All he had to do was finish third or better, and he would become Britain's first World Champion since James Hunt in 1976.

With 63 of the 82 laps completed, Mansell was in third place and dreaming of glory. He entered the high-speed Brabham Straight on lap 64, powering his car up to a scorching 290 kilometres per hour.

Suddenly, his left rear tyre exploded. The rubber shredded instantly whilst the corner of the car buckled. With its tyre gone, the metal wheel ground against the track, producing a spectacular shower of sparks.

Mansell fought wildly to tame his out-of-control car as it bucked and jerked from left to right. Only his supreme driving skill stopped him crashing into other cars or into the wall. He managed to pull the car up safely, but his hopes of the championship were over. Alain Prost, finishing second in the race, would now scoop the title. Mansell would have to wait six more years to become a world champion himself.

NIGEL ERNEST JAMES MANSELL	
Born	1953, Upton-upon-Severn, England
F1 career	1980–92, 1994–95
Total races	192
F1 wins	31

SEVENTH HEAVEN

Winning one F1 World Championship is hard, terribly hard. Winning seven sounds almost impossible, but two men have managed it. Lewis Hamilton was the second, but the first was German legend, Michael Schumacher.

The son of a bricklayer, who later ran his hometown Hürth's go-karting track, Schumacher was a beast. He worked harder than any other driver of his era, both on his car and race tactics, and his mental and physical fitness. Today, all F1 drivers are lean, mean, fitness machines. But during the 1990s, some trained harder than others and some didn't train much at all.

'Schumi' built up his extreme strength and fitness to withstand the huge forces which racing drivers encounter as they speed up, slow down and take tight turns. This meant that his reactions and decisions weren't affected by being exhausted near the end of a crucial race.

After two world championships with Benetton, Schumacher moved to Ferrari. The Italian team hadn't won a title in 21 years, but Schumacher inspired them to new heights and won a truly awe-inspiring and unprecedented five Drivers' World Championships in a row (2000–04).

Schumacher has set many records, including most consecutive seasons of winning one or more F1 races (15 seasons), and the highest number of fastest laps of races achieved by any driver – an incredible 77.

MICHAEL SCHUMACHER	
Born	1969, Hürth, Germany
F1 career	1991–2006, 2010–12
Total races	308
F1 wins	91

FIVE-TIME FANGIO

The early decades of Formula 1 rarely saw people hotly debate who was the best driver. Because everyone knew. It was the quiet Argentine, Juan Manuel Fangio.

Fangio had his first taste of motorsport in deadly cross-country races in Argentina in the 1930s. He was almost forty years old when the F1 World Championship began in 1950, but the following year he became the man to beat.

Juan Manuel Fangio won the 1951 World Championship driving for Alfa before switching to Maserati. A terrible accident at the Formula Two Monza Grand Prix in 1952 saw him break his neck, and he didn't return until part of the way through the 1953 season.

Fangio was nicknamed 'The Maestro' with good reason. He had a brilliant racing mind and knew how to get the most out of whatever car he was driving. He switched teams often and won his second and third World Championships with Mercedes (1954, 1955) before moving to Ferrari and winning a fourth title in 1956.

Switching teams again to Maserati, Fangio won his fifth World Championship in 1957, setting a record still to be beaten: he remains the only driver to win World Championships with four different race teams.

Fangio's statistics are still amazing. He won an incredible 24 of the just over 50 grand prix he started – a record win percentage of 47 per cent. This puts him far ahead of the pack – Max Verstappen's win percentage is 30 per cent and Lewis Hamilton's 29 per cent.

JUAN MANUEL FANGIO	
Born	1911, Balcarce, Argentina
F1 career	1950–51, 1953–58
Total races	52
F1 wins	24

BROTHERS BEYOND

The son of a sports commentator, Emerson Fittipaldi dreamed of racing in Formula 1 from a young age. So did his brother, Wilson Jr. At the time, F1 wasn't big in Brazil and the country didn't have a grand prix of their own.

In 1972, both Fittipaldi brothers entered Formula 1 – Wilson Jr for the Brabham team and Emerson for Lotus. Wilson Jr had some success but was eclipsed by his brother.

Emerson Fittipaldi had a brilliant 1972 season. He was extremely fast. Sometimes, opponents just couldn't keep up with him! He won five of the twelve races and was crowned Brazil's first World Champion. At the time, he was also the youngest champ, just 25 years old.

In 1973 the Brazilian Grand Prix became part of the world championship. And Fittipaldi became a national hero when he won the race. His second world championship came the following year, by which time he was driving for McLaren.

Fittipaldi's fame spread across Brazil and helped spark a huge surge of interest in F1 there. He finished second in the championship in 1975 before spending his last five seasons in F1 in a newly formed Fittipaldi race team with its founder – namely his brother.

EMERSON FITTIPALDI	
Born	1946, São Paulo, Brazil
F1 career	1970–80
Total races	149
F1 wins	14

FORMULA 1 GREATEST MOMENTS

TOTAL DOMINANCE

Red Bull were confident when they rolled out their new RB19 car for the 2023 season. They were pleased with its design and performance. They hoped it would prove a great ride for their drivers, Max Verstappen and Sergio Pérez.

They weren't wrong!

Out of 22 races in the 2023 season, Red Bull won 21 of them. Only Carlos Sainz Jr's victory in Singapore stopped a clean sweep. Of Red Bull's 21 victories, 19 were Max Verstappen's. He was in unstoppable form and led races for more than one thousand laps.

Verstappen's final score in the championship was ridiculous. His 575 points put him 290 points ahead of his teammate, Sergio Pérez. In short, Verstappen had the most commanding lead in any F1 season of the modern era.

POLE STORIES

Being the fastest in qualifying gets you the best starting place for a grand prix: at the front of the grid in pole position. Lewis Hamilton has scored 104 poles; no one else comes close.

Being on pole is no guarantee of victory, but it usually gives you a very good chance... except in Teo Fabi's case.

This Italian driver produced one of the greatest drives in qualifying at the 1985 German Grand Prix. Racing in an unfancied Toleman car, Fabi scorched round the track to record a time 1.1 seconds faster than anyone else. Amazing!

But from that pole position, Fabi had a poor start in the race itself which undid all his hard work, and he never led the race. He scored two further pole positions that season, in Austria and Italy. In both, though, mechanical problems meant he barely got off the start line. This meant that despite three pole positions, he never led an F1 race, not even for just a lap.

TEODORICO FABI	
Born	1955, Milan, Italy
F1 career	1982, 1984–87
Total races	71
F1 wins	0

DRIVE TO SURVIVE

In March 2019, Netflix viewers started streaming a new TV show about Formula 1 called *Drive to Survive*. It took a behind-the-scenes look into the teams that compete in the sport.

The show contained lots of interviews with drivers and team bosses, such as Toto Wolff of Mercedes and Christian Horner of Red Bull. For the first time, the public got a better idea of the characters in the sport and some of the rivalries.

It proved a big hit. Thousands of people who weren't previously into Formula 1 suddenly became hooked on the human drama, as well as on the amazing racing footage. Small cockpit cameras provided edge-of-the-seat action, as if you were in the car with Lewis Hamilton or Max Verstappen.

Some teams and drivers criticised the show saying it made them look silly or that it hyped up rivalries that didn't really exist. But the show has helped boost TV audiences for the actual grand prix races, especially in America. Most find it great fun to watch.

CLIVE GIFFORD

NO TASTE OF SUCCESS

The Arrows Racing Team took part in Formula 1 between 1978 and 2002. During those 24 years, the team achieved four third places and five second places. But they never managed to win any of the 382 races they took part in.

They certainly didn't lack driving talent. At various times, their drivers included Alan Jones, Riccardo Patrese, Thierry Boutsen and, for the 1997 season, the defending world champion, Damon Hill.

The 1997 Hungarian Grand Prix was the closest they got... and there, they got desperately close.

Hill qualified in third but was up into second before you knew it, overtaking Jacques Villeneuve. He then caught race leader, Michael Schumacher and overtook him on lap 11. Brilliant!

Hill led after 30 laps, then 40, then 50 of the 77-lap race. His lead was building. It reached more than 35 seconds over Villeneuve who had taken second place.

Hill was still in front after 60 laps, then 70 laps. Back in the pits, the Arrows team mechanics and staff held their breath. They were nearly there. Damon had a 33-second lead. Could they finally achieve a grand prix victory?

With just laps to go, the car was losing power. There was a leak in the hydraulics that controlled the car's throttle. He nursed the car round the track but on the very last lap, Villeneuve passed him. Curses!

Hill had to be content with an incredible drive and a precious second place for his team. It was the last podium finish Arrows would ever manage.

DAMON GRAHAM DEVEREUX HILL	
Born	1960, London, England
F1 career	1992–1999
Total races	122
F1 wins	22

THE UNITED STATES SIX

Formula 1 is full of controversy and arguments as teams battle each other for supremacy. They bicker over the rules, enter official complaints and generally argue for all they're worth.

One particular series of simmering disagreements came to a head at the 2005 US Grand Prix. After a problem was found, Michelin advised the seven teams using its tyres not to race. These teams then told F1 organisers they would race but only if track changes were made to reduce the wear on their tyres. Ferrari, who used a different make of tyre, disagreed and so did the organisers. The track would stay the same.

The race looked like it would go ahead normally. All 20 cars paraded around the Indianapolis Motor Speedway track on the formation lap. But as they neared the starting grid, 14 cars pulled off into the pits. They refused to race.

Many in the crowd of around 120,000 booed and jeered on seeing just two Ferraris take their place on the grid with two Jordan cars and two from the Minardi team. During the race, thousands flocked to the ticket office to demand their ticket money back.

The race saw the two Ferraris lap the other four cars to notch up a one-two, but Ferrari drivers Michael Schumacher and Rubens Barrichello didn't celebrate on the podium. They and many others in the sport knew that Formula 1 looked foolish that day.

CLIVE GIFFORD

THE FIRST CONSTRUCTORS' CHAMPION

Do you know who was the first team to win the F1 World Constructors' Championships?

Here's a clue… this competition was first held in 1958. Do you think it was Ferrari or maybe Mercedes, Alfa or Lotus?

In fact, the answer is a short-lived team called Vanwall.

Vanwall had first raced in 1954. It was set up by Tony Vandervell, a factory owner from London, who wanted to create a team to beat the Italian outfits like Ferrari, Maserati and Alfa who were dominating F1 in the 1950s.

Vanwall designed a sleek, powerful car, the VW 5, driven by the team's three excellent drivers. There was the trained dentist and super racer, Tony Brooks;

the ex-mechanic, Stuart Lewis-Evans; and superstar, Stirling Moss. Between them, in the 1958 season, they won six of the nine races they entered.

Furthermore, Moss finished second in the Drivers' Championship, with Brooks third and Lewis-Evans ninth. The total number of points scored by the trio put Vanwall well ahead of Ferrari and Cooper to win the manufacturers' title. Only fourteen other teams, out of over 170 that have taken part in F1, have ever been Constructors champions.

DID NOT FINISH DE CESARIS

Popular and fast but sometimes erratic, Andrea de Cesaris certainly livened up Formula 1 racing in the 1980s and early 1990s. In his first full season, in 1981 with McLaren, he had seven race-ending accidents on track. Race fans quickly nicknamed him 'Andrea de Crasheris'.

Moving first to Alfa and then Ligier, the Italian's misfortune continued. Even if he didn't make a mistake or crash on the track, he suffered reliability problems with his racing car.

Yet he did finish second twice and third three times. He also came very close to winning the 1983 Belgian Grand Prix – before a poor pit stop by his team and an engine failure saw him record yet another DNF (Did Not Finish).

In 1987, he moved to Brabham hoping for a change of fortune. It didn't come – that season, de Cesaris failed to finish 14 of the 16 grand prix. In the remaining two, he failed to qualify (Monaco GP) and finished eighth (Mexican GP).

When he retired in 1994, he had raced for ten different teams and scored championship points with nine of them. Impressive. However, he is also remembered for a record 147 DNFs in his 214 grand prix. That equals a staggering DNF percentage of 70.67 per cent.

ANDREA DE CESARIS	
Born	1959, Rome, Italy
F1 career	1980–94
Total races	214
F1 wins	0

GOING OUT ON A HIGH

Imagine winning ten grand prix races in a single season yet not winning the World Championship. That is what happened to Lewis Hamilton in 2016.

Hamilton's team, Mercedes, was in a brilliant run of form. Their W07 Hybrid car they put on the track didn't always start well, but once it got going tended to be screamingly fast. Of the 42 drives made by the vehicle that season, only three ended in retirements.

Hamilton was the defending world champion but was always behind his teammate, Nico Rosberg in the points table. Rosberg had a scorching start to the season, winning the first four grand prix.

Between them, Hamilton and Rosberg carved up win after win – 19 of the 21 races went their way. There was little to separate them, but every time Hamilton put pressure on the German, he seemed to respond.

Rosberg had made many changes to his driving kit and pre-race preparation for the season. He meditated to keep his focus and worked with sports psychologists to improve his aggression while driving.

The changes paid off. He went into the last race of the season at Abu Dhabi with a twelve-point lead over Hamilton, meaning he could finish third and still become champion. In the end, he finished a comfortable second, became World Champion for the first time, and then promptly retired from Formula 1.

NICO ERIK ROSBERG	
Born	1985, Wiesbaden, Germany
F1 career	2006–16
Total races	206
F1 wins	23

SCHECKTER SUCCEEDS

Jody Scheckter was known to be a strong-minded racing driver. Many in the paddock thought the South African speedster would not do well at a big, strict team like Ferrari, when he joined in 1979. He proved them wrong.

The 1979 season didn't start that well – Ferrari's new car wasn't ready and Scheckter and his teammate Gilles Villeneuve had to race in the previous season's vehicle. Things picked up though as the pair formed a great friendship and racing partnership.

By the time that round 13 of the championship occurred, Ferrari were in pole position. Scheckter led the Driver's Championship comfortably, and the next race was a home one for his team. The famous Monza circuit in Italy would be noisy and dominated by the colour red – tens of thousands of Ferrari-mad fans were present.

Scheckter qualified in third place but pulled a great overtaking move off the start line to race ahead of two Renault cars and into first place. Renault's René Arnoux battled back, overtaking Scheckter on the second lap, only for Scheckter to retake the lead on lap 13.

Gilles Villeneuve had moved up into second and the pair crossed the finish line to give home fans and the Ferrari team a sensational one-two. The points Scheckter scored that day made him the first and, so far, only African F1 World Champion.

JODY DAVID SCHECKTER	
Born	1950, East London, South Africa
F1 career	1972–80
Total races	113
F1 wins	10

DOUBLE TROUBLE

The 2022 British Grand Prix did not go the way most British fans wanted. Their favourite, Lewis Hamilton, eventually finished third. Still, it was a podium place in an otherwise difficult season for the Mercedes driver. It had been his first season in a long, long career where he had not obtained a pole position or won a grand prix.

He did, though, perform the move of the season, thrilling those who saw it.

As the race entered its closing stages, Charles Leclerc and Sergio Pérez were battling crazy-hard for a podium position. On lap 45, the two cars raced side by side, veering across the track. Both were striving to enter turns ahead of the other. This battle was exciting but neither driver noticed Hamilton's Mercedes creeping up on them.

Showing the slickest of moves and perfect timing, Hamilton darted on the inside of both drivers, overtaking both in the blink of an eye. The grandstands roared their appreciation and the commentators gasped. It was an audacious move from one of the sport's greats.

FROM TWO WHEELS TO FOUR

John Surtees was a motorcycling legend. Riding for the Italian MV Agusta team, he won seven World Championships in the 1950s, as well as winning the famous Isle of Man TT race three times in a row.

Thirsting for a new challenge, Surtees switched to four-wheeled racing in 1960 with the Lotus F1 team and made an immediate impact. He finished second in his second ever F1 race, the British Grand Prix, and scored his first of eight pole positions at his third, in Portugal.

In 1963, he moved to Ferrari and the following year found himself in a three-way battle for the Championship with famous drivers Graham Hill and Jim Clark.

Come the last race, in Mexico, Hill had a significant

points lead but suffered a mid-race shunt. Another car crashed into the back of his BRM car, wrecking its exhaust system. As Hill lost power and dropped back, Surtees surged forward. He had no hope of catching the race leader Dan Gurney but that didn't matter.

When he crossed the line in second place, Surtees' points total leapt to 40, one more than Hill's. He'd done it! Surtees became the first and only driver to be crowned both a two-wheeled and a four-wheeled World Champion. Awesome!

JOHN NORMAN SURTEES	
Born	1934, Tatsfield, England
F1 career	1960–72
Total races	113
F1 wins	6

SPEED KING

Built in 1922, north of Milan in Italy, the Monza circuit is known as the Temple of Speed. It consists of some frighteningly fast, long straights which mean that drivers can go at full throttle for at least three-quarters of each lap. Vrmm! Vrmm!

In 2005, Juan Pablo Montoya certainly took advantage of Monza's pace. The Colombian driver was in the cockpit of the powerful McLaren MP4-20 car when it arrived for testing, prior to the Italian Grand Prix.

Around the track are sensors called speed traps. These electronic devices measure just how fast the cars are going as they speed by; F1 cars today are too fast for someone holding a stopwatch!

Montoya's race pace was frighteningly good, but even the most experienced F1 technician was surprised when they saw the speed trap measurements: Montoya's car had been clocked at 372.6 km/h. That's more than three times the UK speed limit on motorways. It still stands as the fastest speed travelled by a race specification F1 car.

But it's still not quite the fastest any F1 car has gone. In 2006, Honda took their RA106 car, fitted with different tyres, to the Bonneville Salt Flats in America. There, test driver Alan van der Merwe put the pedal to the metal and reached a mindboggling speed of 397.36 km/h.

JUAN PABLO MONTOYA	
Born	1975, Bogotá, Colombia
F1 career	2001–06
Total races	95
F1 wins	7

THE BAREFOOT BEAR

Denny Hulme was a rare thing in Formula 1 – a driver that didn't like the fame and attention! He had learned to drive on his family's farm in Te Puke in New Zealand at the age of six. As a young man, he moved to Europe to compete in Formula Junior. There, he amazed his opponents by racing in bare feet, which he said gave him a better feel of the accelerator, clutch and brake pedals.

Hulme was big and looked rugged. He was a gruff man, who didn't like chatting, mixing with celebrities or talking to the media. He just liked racing and racing fast. People in the motor racing world started calling him 'The Bear'.

Hulme moved up the motorsports ladder and by 1965, he found himself in Formula 1. He was racing for the Brabham team but even then, he didn't become well known for a while. His first of eight grand prix wins came in 1967 at Monaco. As he was walking towards where he would receive his winner's trophy, the director of the race scurried up to him and, looking a little embarrassed, asked, 'Erm, by the way, monsieur, what is your name?'

The Bear won again at the German Grand Prix and proved a reliable source of points for the Brabham team all season with six more podium finishes. After coming third at the Mexican Grand Prix, in the Drivers' Championship Hulme actually beat his employer, Jack Brabham into second place – which was a little awkward! The Bear was now New Zealand's first F1 World Champion.

DENIS CLIVE HULME	
Born	1936, Motueka, New Zealand
F1 career	1965–74
Total races	112
F1 wins	8

CLIVE GIFFORD

A RETURN TO AFRICA

The F1 World Championship calendar is never permanent. Some races get dropped from the World Championship while new locations get the chance to shine.

F1 has gained grand prix in Miami and Las Vegas, but lost grand prix in Malaysia, India and in 2026, the Netherlands – Max Verstappen's home country.

The last time that Africa saw a Formula 1 grand prix was in 1993 at the Kyalami circuit in South Africa. It was a race remembered for Alain Prost winning in his first drive with the Williams team. Apart from a one-off grand prix in Morocco in 1958, won by Stirling Moss, the only grand prix events to occur on the African continent were all held at tracks in South Africa.

Thirty F1 drivers have come from the continent, so

surely one of the sport's 24 grand prix each year can be held somewhere there? South Africa, Rwanda and Nigeria are all leading candidates to host such an event.

Thousands of African race fans have petitioned F1 organisers and they have received support from a number of F1 drivers including Lewis Hamilton. Hamilton said in August 2024, 'We can't be adding races in other locations and continuing to ignore Africa, which the rest of the world just takes from.'

FANS FOR THE MEMORIES

Formula 1 vehicles are at the cutting edge of technology. Some F1 innovations – like carbon fibre which reduces weight, and gear-changing paddles on the steering wheel – find their way into regular cars years later.

One innovation that didn't make it, though, was a giant fan fitted to the back of a car. The car was a Brabham BT46B and the year was 1978. The fan was designed to suck air away from underneath the vehicle. This would create downforce to help the car to grip the track and allow it to take turns at higher speeds.

When Brabham took their 'fan car' to the Swedish Grand Prix, they covered the large fan with a dustbin lid whilst in the pits. But out on the track, the fan was clearly visible. John Watson, who was driving one BT46B, spun off during the nineteenth lap of the race. But the other BT46B, driven by Niki Lauda, won comfortably, by more than 34 seconds.

Other teams protested, furious at the innovation but the authorities said it was not against the rules and the win stood. The Brabham team, though, decided not to race it again, so it was retired with a perfect record: Races: one; Wins: one.

THE FLYING SCOT

Jim Clark could race any type of car and do it really well. In 1965, the Scotsman became the first non-American driver for 49 years to win the Indy 500 race. He also won sports and touring car races and managed to win the Formula 1 World Championship twice.

But Clark drove cars that were often unreliable. Mechanical problems forced him to retire from 28 grand prix races, yet his smooth, fast driving saw him win 25 of the remainder. That's an incredible achievement. And he is talked about as being as good as greats of the sport like Juan Manuel Fangio and Ayrton Senna.

One of Clark's most memorable performances occurred at the 1963 Belgian GP. He started in eighth position, but after less than a quarter of a lap, had powered his way to first. The rain came pouring down, making the track highly slippery. Consequently, some drivers faltered and some team bosses pleaded with the organisers to stop the race.

But Clark just kept on driving his Lotus fast, despite a gearbox problem. He held the gear stick in position with one hand and the bottom of the steering wheel with the other to stop the car sliding away as he took the tight turns of the Spa track. He finished an incredible 4 minutes and 54 seconds ahead of second-placed Bruce McLaren. It was a stunning drive by the flying Scot.

JAMES CLARK	
Born	1936, Kilmany, Scotland
F1 career	1960–68
Total races	73
F1 wins	25

CLIVE GIFFORD

TERRIBLE START, AWESOME FINISH

For many F1 fans, the start of a grand prix is their favourite part of the race. The expectation as the drivers rev their engines, the drama as the cars pull away and the excitement as the cars battle for position around the first lap – it's like nothing else.

Some starts in F1 history have been chaotic. Take the 1998 Belgian GP, for instance. The weather was terrible, but the start was even worse. David Coulthard lost control of his McLaren, bounced off the trackside wall back across the track and triggered a thirteen-car pile-up! It took more than an hour to clear all the expensive F1 car debris. Thankfully, no one was seriously injured.

> 'Oh, this is terrible, this is quite appalling, this is the worst start to a Grand Prix I have ever seen in the whole of my life.'
> – Murray Walker, BBC commentator.

Even after the restart, there was some further trouble. Mika Häkkinen and Johnny Herbert collided and were out of the race. Then Alexander Wurz and David Coulthard tangled, and a little later, Michael Schumacher rammed the back of Coulthard's car. Schumacher then had a tantrum back in the pits.

Soon, only eight cars were left – amongst them, both bright yellow vehicles of the unfancied Jordan team. Damon Hill took the chequered flag to finish first, with his teammate, Ralf Schumacher, second. It was Jordan's 126th race and their first ever grand prix victory.

A HALF POINT TO PROVE

Come the start of the 1975 F1 season, all eyes were on the last placed car on the grid for the South African Grand Prix. Its driver was the Italian, Lella Lombardi – the first woman to qualify for a grand prix since 1958.

Lombardi's race only lasted 23 laps before her car broke down with a fuel system problem. But in her next race, in Barcelona, she drove her March car to a brilliant sixth place. She finished ahead of three male drivers who would all become world champions: James Hunt, Jody Scheckter and Niki Lauda.

The race was greatly shortened due to accidents. As a result, half the normal race points were awarded to the top drivers. Lombardi received half a point towards the Drivers' World Championship.

Frustratingly, Lombardi had to retire in the next two

races – in Belgium and Sweden – before she notched up another excellent finish, this time seventh place at the German Grand Prix. It put her just out of contention for points (at that time only awarded to the top six drivers) but ahead of drivers like Mario Andretti and James Hunt.

Lombardi qualified for a total of twelve races in 1975 and 1976 but didn't manage to finish in the top ten again. So, she had to be content with her half a point, which made her the only woman to ever score points in the F1 Drivers' World Championship.

MARIA GRAZIA 'LELLA' LOMBARDI	
Born	1941, Frugarolo, Italy
F1 career	1974–76
Total races	17
F1 wins	0

CLIVE GIFFORD

WIN BY A WHISKER

The 1971 Italian Grand Prix at Monza is remembered for a thrilling finish, the closest in F1 history.

Six drivers were racing neck and neck as the Grand Prix entered its closing stages. Unlucky Chris Amon suddenly lost his helmet visor, making it five at the front: François Cevert, Ronnie Peterson, Howden Ganley, Peter Gethin and Mike Hailwood.

At the start of the final lap, Gethin – driving a McLaren – was in fourth place. Somehow, he weaved his way into second place just behind Peterson. At the final corner, all the cars, their engines screaming, tried to get to the front. Together, they crossed the line in a blur.

A mere 0.18 seconds separated the first four cars. Hailwood was fourth, Cevert third and Peterson second. Gethin won by the tiniest of margins – just 0.01 or one-hundredth of a second. It was his first and only grand prix win.

PETER KENNETH GETHIN	
Born	1940, Ewell, England
F1 career	1970–74
Total races	31
F1 wins	1

MAD MAX

Max Verstappen was fuming after the 2023 Singapore Grand Prix. He had finished fifth, not the worst result in the world, but for Verstappen it was unacceptable. He described driving the car as 'a shocking experience'.

The defending world champion was grumpy because he was a perfectionist. And in 2023, he was having as close to a perfect season as was possible. Before Singapore, he had won a record ten grand prix in a row. After Singapore, he won every race left in the season.

Verstappen's record in 2023 was extraordinary. Singapore was the only race in which he didn't finish first or second. He won 19 of the 22 grand prix that season and ended with a record 575 points, more than double that of his teammate, Sergio Pérez.

Sure, F1 today awards more points than in the past, but

a better measure of Verstappen's supremacy is how in 2023 he scored almost 93 per cent of the maximum points available. No one else in F1 history comes close.

FUEL FOR THOUGHT

In 1982, the Brabham team started a new tactic of starting races with insufficient fuel to go the distance. Their cars were much lighter and faster as a result, even allowing for the time lost to come into the pits to refuel. Many teams followed Brabham's strategy – until the FIA banned refuelling in 1984.

Refuelling was permitted once again in F1 for the 1994 season and proved to be a crucial part of strategy. Teams had to balance fuel with weight, as well as stress on tyres and engines. It made pit stops and race strategy more like chess matches. Some fans loved it; others thought it detracted from real racing.

There were several memorable refuelling accidents that, thankfully, saw no loss of life. Jos Verstappen, Max Verstappen's dad, was surrounded by fire when fuel was sprayed on the hot bodywork of his car at the

1994 German GP.

Fifteen years later, at the Brazilian Grand Prix in São Paulo, Heikki Kovalainen drove away from his pit stop with the fuel hose still attached. It sprayed rival driver Kimi Räikkönen with fuel which then caught fire, engulfing the driver in flames. Luckily, both drivers were able to continue the race.

Refuelling was banned again in 2010 due to cost – mobile refuelling rigs cost a lot of money – and for safety reasons. Some people would like to see it return, but it is thought unlikely.

FEMALE-FREE GRID

Since the memorable moments of Lella Lombardi in the 1970s, no woman has raced in a grand prix. A handful have tried, though, including the British professional skier, Divina Gallica; the South African racer, Desiré Wilson; and the Italian Formula 3000 driver Giovanna Amati.

Sadly, none of these three contenders posted a fast enough time in qualifying to enter the race proper. On one occasion, Wilson did manage to qualify for a Formula 1 race, but not one that was part of the F1 World Championship.

It was for the British Formula 1 Championship, which ran from 1978 to 1982, and which featured cars built to F1 rules, and racing on a series of race tracks around Britain. In 1980, Wilson qualified for the second race of the season, held at the famous Brands

Hatch circuit. She was driving a four-year-old Wolf WR3 car, but didn't let that bother her as she stormed to victory. Outstanding!

It made Wilson the only woman to win a Formula 1 race of any kind. She also finished second at Thruxton and third at the Mallory Park circuit. A grandstand at Brands Hatch was later named in her honour.

DESIRÉ WILSON	
Born	1953, Brakpan, South Africa
F1 career	1980
Total races	0
F1 wins	0

THAT WINNING FEELING

Lewis Hamilton has little left to prove in Formula 1. The seven-times champion is a legend for the impact he has made both on and off the track.

In 2020, in the Portuguese Grand Prix at Portimão, Hamilton notched up his ninety-second GP win, taking him past the total of previous record holder, Michael Schumacher. In 2021, at the Russian Grand Prix in Sochi and one of eight wins he enjoyed that year, Hamilton's tally of grand prix victories reached one hundred.

Then, suddenly, the winning stopped.

Hamilton went through all of 2022 and 2023 without finishing first. It was something he was not used to. What made it harder for him to bear was seeing his great rival, Max Verstappen on the winner's podium again and again.

He kept his focus and worked hard with the Mercedes team to improve the car which was not performing at a high enough level. But he also had doubts whether, at 39 years old, he was still good enough.

Nevertheless, Hamilton always received amazing support during the British Grand Prix, and in 2024, he sent the crowds wild by fighting off attacks by Max Verstappen to cross the line first. It was his record ninth victory at Silverstone and the normally ice-cool icon shed tears on the podium.

The 945-day wait was over. Lewis Hamilton was a winner again.

DOING DOUGHNUTS

In 2013, Sebastian Vettel was unstoppable. He had reeled off a staggering nine grand prix wins that season, before the Indian Grand Prix, held at the Buddh International Circuit.

Vettel led the race from the off but made a surprise early pit stop which saw him suddenly down to seventeenth place. Had his Red Bull team lost the plot? The answer was a resounding NO!

He started carving up the cars in front of him, overtaking one then another as he moved up the field. His Red Bull RB9 was speeding along majestically under his control. By lap 28 of the 60-lap race, he was back in the lead. Even with a second pit stop three laps later, he remained in control.

Vettel finished the race nearly 30 seconds ahead of

runner-up Nico Rosberg. Not only was it his tenth race win of the season – it also guaranteed him his fourth World Championship. At the time, only three other drivers (Fangio, Schumacher and Prost) had won four titles, and at the age of 26, Vettel was much younger than any of them.

He celebrated his victory with a series of eye-catching doughnuts – tight spins on the track – which sent huge clouds of smoke up into the air. Then, he knelt and bowed down in front of his car, before heading over to the track barriers and throwing his gloves into the crowd. It was a memorable celebration by a driver at his peak.

SEBASTIAN VETTEL	
Born	1987, Heppenheim, Germany
F1 career	2007–22
Total races	300
F1 wins	53

NEVER A DULL MOMENT

The 1977 British Grand Prix saw the F1 debut of the 1974 World Snowmobile Derby champion. Gilles Villeneuve was a Canadian who had begun racing in his souped-up old Ford Mustang in local drag races in Quebec, then competed in dozens of snowmobile races.

The move from skis, snow and ice to hot rubber and racetracks didn't faze Villeneuve. He quickly wowed fans with his daring racing and his sheer speed. The young Canadian was fast and loved overtaking.

Villeneuve's peak came in 1979, with his second full season in Formula 1. His profile soared, with memorable battles on the track against top drivers like Alan Jones, Nelson Piquet and René Arnoux. His tussles against Arnoux were especially memorable (see p. 123). He also had enough crashes for his team boss, Enzo Ferrari, to nickname him 'the Prince of Destruction'.

During 1979, Villeneuve won three races and finished second in three more. He even led the championship just before the midway point, but before the last race of the season, his teammate Jody Scheckter had won the World Championship.

Villeneuve could have been downhearted and slow. Instead, he chose to be deadly focused and unbelievably fast. In practise at the Watkins Glen circuit, he was many seconds faster than any other driver. He won the race at a canter despite having a problem with the oil pressure in his engine for 25 laps or so. He won by more than 48 seconds, having lapped many of the other drivers.

JOSEPH GILLES HENRI VILLENEUVE	
Born	1950, Saint-Jean-sur-Richelieu, Canada
F1 career	1977–82
Total races	68
F1 wins	6

COURAGEOUS COMEBACK

At the 1976 German Grand Prix, Niki Lauda came close to death. His Ferrari had crashed horribly at the Nürburgring. The car burst into flames with him still trapped in his cockpit. It took the bravery of other drivers, including Brett Lunger and Arturo Merzario, to pluck him from the blazing wreck.

Lauda was terribly injured, his lungs damaged and his head covered in severe burns. It was thought he would not make it through his first night in hospital. Yet, 40 days later, he was climbing into his Ferrari car wearing a specially modified helmet to fit over his bandaged head.

Drivers, mechanics and race fans could only marvel at his bravery and determination to get back in an F1 car so soon. For Lauda, it was simple. He had been leading the World Championship before his crash, had only missed two races and wanted to get back and compete for the title.

Despite being in terrible pain, Lauda completed the Grand Prix at Monza, finishing fourth and gaining three World Championship points. His story made world news and attracted many new fans to the sport. But ultimately he lost out on the 1976 championship by just one agonising point, to British driver, James Hunt.

The following season, still in pain from his injuries, Lauda put his setbacks behind him to triumph. He became World Champion for a second time. A third championship win would follow in 1984, putting him up with the greats.

ANDREAS NIKOLAUS 'NIKI' LAUDA	
Born	1949, Vienna, Austria
F1 career	1971–79, 1982–85
Total races	177
F1 wins	25

CUTTING CORNERS

Harry Schell had taken part in a number of grand prix races during the 1950s. But the American driver had never really excelled and hadn't come close to achieving pole position or a race win. Yet he was popular with fans for driving flamboyantly and taking risks. He was also a practical joker. 'You always had to watch your back with Harry,' said fellow US driver, Carroll Shelby.

In 1959, Schell's fortunes in F1 improved. As part of the BRM team, he scored five championship points and was enjoying his best season. But then he participated in the United States Grand Prix, held at Sebring, an airfield converted into a racetrack, and people simply couldn't believe the qualifying lap he put in.

Schell's lap time of 3 minutes 5.2 seconds was some six seconds faster than he had previously achieved at Sebring – a huge improvement. His time knocked the leading Ferrari back into fourth – and the Italian team were furious! It placed Schell third alongside racing legends Stirling Moss and Jack Brabham right at the front of the grid.

Only after the race had finished did the reason for Schell's amazing improvement became known – he had cheated! He had spotted an escape road at the back of the circuit that joined up to a later part of the track. It was a shortcut, and Schell took it to slash his lap time.

In the 1950s, there were far fewer cameras around and spectators weren't allowed at the rear of the circuit, so Schell's move went unnoticed. His cheating didn't impact on the race though. Firstly, he slipped down to eighth on the first lap then his clutch broke on the sixth lap, forcing him to retire.

HARRY LAWRENCE O'REILLY SCHELL	
Born	1921, Paris, France
F1 career	1950–60
Total races	57
F1 wins	0

GIVE TEENS A CHANCE

What do most teenagers want for their eighteenth birthday present? How about a drive in a Formula 1 car for one of the sport's leading teams?

In August 2024, that's what the Italian teenager, Andrea Kimi Antonelli got. Mercedes team boss, Toto Wolff confirmed the youngster would take a Mercedes car out at practice before the Italian Grand Prix. Three years earlier, Antonelli had still been go-karting, before making a quick move into Formula Four then Formula Two racing.

His practice experience didn't last long. After some notably quick laps, he misjudged the turn into the Parabolica corner and thumped into the rows of tyres that act as a safety barrier. CRUNCH! Antonelli was unharmed.

FORMULA 1 GREATEST MOMENTS

Any disappointment at his opportunity being cut short didn't last long. Lewis Hamilton was leaving Mercedes for Ferrari, and Antonelli was selected to take his place – to race for Mercedes alongside George Russell for the 2025 season.

'It is an amazing feeling,' Antonelli said during the announcement. 'Reaching F1 is a dream I've had since I was a small boy.'

ANDREA KIMI ANTONELLI	
Born	2006, Bologna, Italy
F1 career	2025–
Total races	1
F1 wins	0

WONDERFUL ONE-TWO

The McLaren team had a nightmare in qualifying for the 1983 United States Grand Prix West. They couldn't get their cars balanced to race fast around the bumpy Long Beach circuit. John Watson found himself twenty-second on the starting grid, with his teammate Niki Lauda in twenty-third.

Instead of being downhearted, both Watson and Lauda were determined and confident of moving up the field. The team's mechanics had been working flat out, and both drivers knew their cars would be fast and competitive once they had warmed up and raced plenty of laps.

Lauda got ahead of Watson at the start as the pair began working their way through the field. Their McLaren MP4 cars were performing well. By lap 28, only three cars were ahead of the pair. On lap 32,

Watson got ahead of Lauda and on lap 45, when in second, he attacked the race leader, Jacques Laffite. He darted inside Laffite's car, hitting the brakes as late as possible to get ahead. Watson took the lead, a quite unthinkable prospect at the race's start.

With 30 laps to go, there was plenty to focus on, but Watson drove smoothly and rapidly. He took the chequered flag with a lead of more than 28 seconds over his teammate for a memorable one-two for McLaren. No other driver has come from so far back to win an F1 race.

JOHN MARSHALL WATSON	
Born	1946, Belfast, Northern Ireland
F1 career	1973–83, 1985
Total races	154
F1 wins	5

CLIVE GIFFORD

A GREAT BATTLE

Sometimes, the greatest moments in a Formula 1 race or season aren't about gaining the lead. At the 1979 French Grand Prix, one of the tightest, most enthralling battles was for second place, behind the winner, Jean-Pierre Alain Jabouille.

Cheered on by his home crowd, René Arnoux in a Renault was in third place and chasing Gilles Villeneuve in his Ferrari. On lap 71, with just nine laps to go, Arnoux set the fastest lap of the day, over one full second quicker than the next car.

Five laps later, and Arnoux was right behind Villeneuve. What followed was epic racing, with the pair passing each other again and again. Their cars made contact three times in as many laps but stayed on the track. It was a dazzling display of driving skill, competitive nerve and split-second reactions.

There was nothing to separate them as they headed into the last lap. As they reached the very last corner, the two were racing side-by-side. It was thrilling and too close to call. Suddenly, Villeneuve lurched fractionally ahead. He crossed the line less than a quarter of a second ahead of Arnoux.

Both drivers were proud of their efforts. 'It's my best memory of grand prix racing,' Villeneuve would later recall. 'I am not sad to be third,' grinned Arnoux straight after the race. 'Gilles drove a fantastic race. I enjoyed it very much!'

RENÉ ALEXANDRE ARNOUX	
Born	1948, Pontcharra, France
F1 career	1978–89
Total races	165
F1 wins	7

LAP MASTER

The last grand prix of the 2024 season was notable for several reasons. It marked the last drive for Lewis Hamilton in a Mercedes car – the single most successful partnership in F1 history. It also saw Lando Norris notch up his fourth grand prix win, while his team, McLaren, won their first Constructors' Championship in 26 years.

While Norris began his celebrations, Fernando Alonso in his Aston Martin cruised quietly over the line in ninth place. He gained two points for his team but also set an extraordinary record: no other driver had raced so many grand prix laps as the Spanish veteran.

Since his debut at the 2001 Australian Grand Prix, Alonso has raced an incredible 21,827 laps. That's 107,949 kilometres, or more than two-and-a-half times around Earth. When you add in all the laps driven in qualifying and practice, Alonso has completed a staggering 72,570 laps. That's more than 360,000 kilometres or the distance between Earth and the Moon!

During his career, Alonso has won 32 races, two World Championships and secured 106 podium finishes. He has scored an incredible 2,339 points so far. Astonishingly, at 43 years of age, he intends to continue racing with Aston Martin so there may be more points and certainly more laps in store for the Spanish legend.

FERNANDO ALONSO DIAZ	
Born	1981, Oviedo, Spain
F1 career	2001–19, 2021–
Total races	405
F1 wins	32

CLIVE GIFFORD

RACE DAY MIX-UPS

The organisers at the 1977 Austrian Grand Prix were left red-faced when the podium celebrations began after the race. Try as they might, they couldn't find a copy of the Australian national anthem to play to celebrate Australian driver Alan Jones's win that day. It was a time long before streaming music services or thousands of music tracks stored on computer.

So, they improvised – and when Jones stood on the podium and looked up at the Australian flag, the speakers blared out 'Happy Birthday'. It wasn't even his birthday!

And it certainly hasn't been the only mistake made on a race day.

At the 1985 British Grand Prix, Alain Prost was shown the chequered flag on lap 65, signalling he had won.

The only problem was that the race was supposed to be 66 laps long.

In modern times, with electronic timing and screens, you'd think such mistakes wouldn't be possible. But you'd be wrong! The 2018 Canadian Grand Prix and the 2019 Chinese Grand Prix both ended one lap short. Oops!

HUNT THE SHUNT

James Hunt was a daredevil racer who quickly won the hearts of British race fans. He took risks, he riled other drivers, and he was fast – sometimes dangerously so.

He had earned his nickname of 'Hunt the Shunt' for having lots of accidents in lower classes of racing before he joined the Hesketh F1 racing team. With their teddy-bear badge and their reputation for partying, Hesketh were seen as a bit of a joke… until they started qualifying and finishing high up the grid.

Hunt gained podium finishes in all three seasons as a Hesketh driver, with his first grand prix victory at the 1975 Dutch Grand Prix. He then switched teams to McLaren for the following season, which featured an edge-of-the-seat battle between Hunt and Niki Lauda.

Surprisingly, the carefree Hunt and the analytical, serious Lauda were great friends. Lauda admired Hunt as a superb, natural driver, while Hunt was envious of Lauda's great technical skills. Lauda built up a daunting lead in the championship, but then had a terrible crash (see p. 115) and was out for two races. Hunt won six races to keep pace with the great Austrian.

It all came down to the last race of the season in Japan where rainswept conditions and a new track made racing gripping for fans but terrifying for drivers. Lauda was unable to blink because of his crash injuries and retired during the race. Hunt battled on to finish third, and pipped Lauda to the World Championship by just one point. No British driver would be World Champion again until Nigel Mansell triumphed in 1992.

JAMES SIMON WALLIS HUNT	
Born	1947, Belmont, England
F1 career	1973–79
Total races	93
F1 wins	10

MANSELL MANIA

Nigel Mansell was a huge favourite of British race fans. His attacking style which included lots of daring overtaking moves made him a hero to many. Many fans remembered how he was cruelly denied the 1986 World Championship. So, they were bound to urge him on when he took part in his home grand prix at Silverstone in 1992.

Mansell entered the British Grand Prix in great spirits, having won the first five races of the season, already establishing a commanding lead in the World Championship. His qualifying time at the British GP stunned opponents – it was over two seconds faster than anyone else.

A grand slam is a relatively rare event in Formula 1. It is when a driver starts the race in pole position, leads every lap and records the fastest lap of the entire race.

But Mansell achieved a slam at the race, cheered on by the huge crowd.

Thousands spilled onto the track with joy. Mansell struggled to get back to his team as he got caught up in the crowd. To make his day even better, this victory was his twenty-eighth F1 win, meaning he had passed Jackie Stewart's record number of wins by a British driver.

DOING A "SHOEY"

There have been some epic celebrations by F1 drivers exhilarated either by winning or getting on the podium. The Australian driver, Daniel Ricciardo waited until his thirteenth podium, at the 2016 German Grand Prix, to perform a particularly memorable celebration.

While the other drivers sprayed champagne about, he took off his racing shoe, poured champagne into it, and then drank using the footwear as a cup. Urgh! You've got to bear in mind that during a race, a driver will lose two to three kilograms of weight in sweat alone… Double Urgh!

Furthermore, Ricciardo decided it wouldn't be a one-off. He performed a 'shoey' twice more in 2016. At the Belgian Grand Prix, he coaxed fellow driver, Mark Webber into taking a sip. At the Malaysia Grand Prix,

Nico Rosberg, Max Verstappen and Red Bull team boss, Christian Horner all had a drink from Ricciardo's shoe.

DANIEL JOSEPH RICCIARDO	
Born	1989, Perth, Australia
F1 career	2011–24
Total races	258
F1 wins	8

DRIVER ERROR

Mistakes sometimes happen in the pit lanes when F1 cars come in for new tyres or repairs. In 2007, Kazuki Nakajima was racing in his first ever grand prix, at the Interlagos circuit in Brazil. On lap 39, his Williams team came over the radio to call him into the pits.

It was the last race of the season, and Nakajima had got the drive after Alexander Wurz retired. Nakajima's dad, Satoru, had been an F1 driver, competing in 74 grand prix between 1987 and 1991. Understandably, his son was desperate to impress.

Nakajima slipped off the track and into the pit lane, but he raced to his team in the pits a little too fast. As he drove into position, he knocked two of his team's pit crew over. Ouch! Fortunately, neither were injured badly.

Nakajima went on to finish tenth and got to apologise to his team's mechanics. His pit-stop skills may not have impressed, but his lap times did. The Williams team selected him to be one of their two drivers for the next two seasons. He would race in 36 grand prix.

DARK DAYS

Formula 1 is safer now than it has ever been. In the past things were different – drivers, teams and fans alike knew that one major mistake could have terrible consequences.

The 1994 San Marino Grand Prix is forever remembered as a dark weekend for the sport. During qualifying for what would have been his third grand prix, Roland Ratzenberger died in a high-speed impact when his MTV Simtek car, travelling at 315 kilometres per hour, crashed.

Race organisers decided to continue with the race weekend. Some drivers, like Ayrton Senna, thought about pulling out but lined up for the race. More tragedy was to unfold.

Senna was leading the race on lap seven as he

approached Tamburello, a high-speed corner. His car careered off the track and struck a concrete wall. The three-time world champion died, leaving F1 in grief. His funeral in the Brazilian city of São Paulo was attended by more than half a million people.

Only one driver has since died due to an accident at a grand prix weekend – in 2014, Jules Bianchi crashed on the Suzuka track during the Japanese Grand Prix, and died from his injuries after nine months in a coma. The number 17, Bianchi's race number, was retired from Formula 1 in his honour.

SCHMITZ'S STRATEGY

It's a great source of sadness that there are no female drivers currently racing in Formula 1. But that doesn't mean there aren't women in positions of power and importance in the sport. In the recent past there have been team bosses like Claire Williams (of Williams) and Monisha Kaltenborn (of Sauber) who ran the day-to-day operations of an F1 team.

Today, women including Laura Müller work as race engineers (in her case, for Haas) – or, like Hannah Schmitz at Red Bull, as Principal Strategy Engineers, a crucial role which analyses all the car and race data to decide on racing strategy for each driver. Decisions made include tyre use, when to maintain pace or attack, when to call pit stops, and much more besides.

Schmitz works closely with Max Verstappen and is credited with making the difference in several of his races. These include the 2019 Brazilian GP where she made the brave decision to bring Verstappen in for a third pit stop knowing it would lose him the lead at that point. But that strategic move helped Verstappen win the race.

At the 2022 Hungarian Grand Prix, Schmitz made a bold call not to use hard tyres on Verstappen's car, even though his rivals were racing on them. The decision helped him go from tenth to first place and secure his twenty-eighth grand prix victory.

Straight after the race, Verstappen praised Schmitz. 'Today, I think Hannah, our strategist, was insanely calm. Yeah, she's very good.'

DRIVING AT NIGHT

In 2008, something pretty amazing happened in the already amazing world of Formula 1... the drivers raced in the middle of the night.

With the Singapore Grand Prix about to debut, it was decided that it would be too hot for the cars, drivers, mechanics and spectators to race in the middle of the day. So, the Marina Bay Street Circuit was lined with nearly 1,500 powerful light projectors to illuminate the track, pits and surrounding area.

The circuit was excellent, and the first race was certainly eventful, particularly for Brazilian Felipe Massa. He led and was looking good for the win – until he had a pit stop mishap. He accelerated away from his pit crew, with the fuel pipe still dangling from his car's tank and spraying fuel all over the place.

His pit crew chased him down the pit lane and removed it, but Massa had lost vital time. He eventually finished thirteenth, more than 35 seconds behind the winner, Fernando Alonso.

Some drivers moaned about the track being bumpy, but most team bosses were impressed by the new circuit and its facilities. In short, the Singapore Grand Prix and racing at night was a success. There are now night races at many new grand prix locations in the Middle East including Qatar, Abu Dhabi and Saudi Arabia.

CLIVE GIFFORD

THE POSTHUMOUS WORLD CHAMPION

Dashing driver Jochen Rindt, born in Germany but raised in Austria, grew up idolising Count Wolfgang von Trips, a German racing driver who died tragically at the Monza circuit in 1961.

Rindt was a titan in Formula Two – he won F2 championships in Britain and France – but struggled to get a competitive drive in a Formula 1 car for a while. Finally, in 1969, he gained a seat in the Lotus team who had a great new car, the Lotus 72, for him the following season.

The Lotus 72 and Rindt proved to be a great partnership. He won the Monaco Grand Prix before amassing a run of wins in the Netherlands, France, Britain and Germany. With four races to go, Rindt's lead in the Drivers' Championship was enormous when the teams all headed to Monza for the Italian Grand Prix.

During practice for the race, tragedy struck. Rindt crashed heavily as he approached the Parabolica corner. He died on the way to hospital. It was the same turn at which Rindt's great hero, von Trips, had perished. Lotus withdrew their other cars from the race. Formula 1 had lost another popular and talented racer.

At the end of the season, Rindt's 45 points still put him ahead of his nearest rival, Jacky Ickx. So Jochen Rindt became the only driver to be crowned F1 World Champion after his death.

KARL JOCHEN RINDT	
Born	1942, Mainz, Germany
F1 career	1964–70
Total races	62
F1 wins	6

OH, BROTHER

Between 1997 and 2006, there was not one but two Schumachers on the track in Formula 1. While Michael raced for Ferrari, his younger brother, Ralf, competed for the Jordan, Williams and Toyota teams.

Michael was almost seven years older than Ralf. The big age gap meant that growing up, the two brothers never competed against each other in karting or other classes of racing. It was only in F1 where they got the chance to race head-to-head.

In three of the seasons in which they both raced, Ralf finished fifth in the Drivers' Championship while his brother, was champion. The only season in which Ralf beat his brother, points wise, was in 1999 when he scored 141 and Michael 138.

Between them, the brothers notched up a formidable

1,895 points and 97 grand prix wins. They are the only brothers in history to both score points in F1.

The Schumacher siblings' peak came at the 2001 Canadian Grand Prix. Ralf in his Williams car drove a terrific race. When his brother, leading the race, went into the pits, he raced round the track setting three lap records in a row, to take the lead. Ralf won the race with Michael second. It was Ralf's second grand prix victory and the only time in F1 history that brothers had scored a grand prix one-two.

RALF SCHUMACHER	
Born	1975 Hürth, Germany
F1 career	1997–2007
Total races	182
F1 wins	6

THE HALF-POINT CHAMPION

Niki Lauda retired from Formula 1 in 1979; during practice for the Canadian Grand Prix, he upped and left. As a two-time World Champion, he had nothing to prove. After leaving F1, he went off to start up an airline called Lauda Air.

Lauda had told his team boss, Bernie Ecclestone that he no longer wanted to 'continue the silliness of driving around in circles'. But three years later, he was back, signing to drive for McLaren. He proved he was competitive from the start, winning his second race back, the South African Grand Prix.

Throughout the 1982 season, Lauda's races were either retirements – he was forced to retire from six races – or podium: five wins and four second places.

One of his retirements came at Monaco where he

spun off after just eight laps. His main rival for the title, Alain Prost, won the race, which was stopped after 31 laps due to heavy rain and flooding. So, it was decided that half the normal points would be awarded – meaning that Prost only gained 4½ points for his victory. Those half-points proved crucial: at the end of the season, Lauda had scored 72 points and Prost 71½. It was the smallest margin of victory in F1 history.

Whilst Lauda loved winning, he didn't care much for fame or some of his winners' trophies which he thought were 'ugly'. He gave away many of his trophies to a local garage in Austria, and in return, he received free car washes!

TEARS IN CANADA

At the 1995 Canadian Grand Prix, in fifth place on the starting grid was the popular but win-less Jean Alesi.

He was in his fifth year driving for the Ferrari team and although he had come close, he had never won a grand prix. He was feeling the pressure. It was also his thirty-first birthday and he knew what birthday present he would most like...

Alesi roared off the line and soon passed his teammate, Gerhard Berger to go into fourth place, before zooming past David Coulthard to get into third.

About a quarter of the way into the race, Alesi got in front of Damon Hill. Now he was up into second. Great stuff! Michael Schumacher, though, was a long distance ahead. It would be really hard to catch him. But suddenly, Schumacher's Benetton car limped into the pits, his race over.

Alesi crossed the finish line first and blubbed. Hot tears rolled down his cheeks and smeared his helmet visor. His car promptly ran out of fuel, but he didn't care. He removed his steering wheel, leapt out of the cockpit and stood on top of his car, acting like a surfer until the car rolled to a standstill. The crowd went wild!

JEAN ROBERT ALESI	
Born	1964, Avignon, France
F1 career	1989–2001
Total races	202
F1 wins	1

SMOKING SPORT / BLAZE OF COLOUR

During the 1950s and 1960s, Formula 1 car colour schemes were based on the nationality of their race team. So, Ferrari and other Italian teams had red cars, the cars of French teams were painted blue, Belgium yellow, and German teams' cars were either white or unpainted. With red, white and blue already taken, Britain went for green.

In 1968, at the South African Grand Prix, that colour-coding system began to change. A new private team started by Zimbabwean racing driver John Love named itself after its sponsor, Gunston cigarettes. Its cars were decked out in garish orange, brown and gold, the colours of Gunston cigarette cartons.

Many other teams followed suit as the money from sponsorship was welcomed. By the 1980s, money from tobacco companies was one of the main sources of income for F1 teams.

Even though the harmful effects of smoking tobacco were known well before, it wasn't until 2006 that all tobacco advertising was banned on F1 cars. Teams have continued with lots of other sponsors, and all have their own distinctive liveries (or colour schemes) for their cars, race suits, brochures, the works.

Some teams alter liveries during the season to commemorate historic events or simply to grab attention. For the last three races of 2024, for example, the Alpine team cars were painted a shocking pink at the request of their sponsors AWT.

MARVELLOUS MONZA

If you were a British F1 fan in the 1960s, you would have adored the 1965 Italian Grand Prix.
It was held at Monza – a high-speed circuit with long straights that always saw fast racing. The Centro-Sud team sent not two but three cars to take part. So did Lotus, Brabham and Ferrari.

Four British drivers jostled for the lead: John Surtees, Graham Hill, Jim Clark and a rookie, Jackie Stewart, who made his first F1 appearance at Monza. Stewart was a young Scottish driver in the same team as the great Graham Hill. He knew very little about his BRM car or grand prix racing in general. Should he attack or defend his position? How should he look after his brakes and tyres over 76 gruelling laps? He wasn't sure, so just drove as fast as he could.

With just two laps to go in the race, the lead had

already passed between the four different drivers a record 41 times. The forty-second and final change of leader occurred as Hill went a little wide at a turn and Stewart nipped through, past his teammate.

The rookie had won his first grand prix, but certainly not his last. Twenty-six further wins came as Stewart enjoyed a glittering F1 career. He would win the Drivers' World Championship three times (1969, 1971, 1973) and become a sporting icon.

JOHN YOUNG 'JACKIE' STEWART	
Born	1939, Milton, Scotland
F1 career	1965–73
Total races	100
F1 wins	27

THE INCREDIBLE WIN

Long before there was an F1 World Championship, there were grand prix races in Italy, Germany, France and elsewhere. One of the great legends of this early era was the Italian, Tazio Nuvolari.

Nuvolari was short and frail-looking, but absolutely fearless. After winning a race in 1933, he was asked what he thought of his new car's brakes. He replied that he couldn't tell, as he hadn't really used them!

Driving in all sorts of cars, Nuvolari won 50 major races between 1927 and 1950, including 24 grand prix. But one of his most stirring victories came at the 1935 German Grand Prix.

At the time, German vehicle-makers Auto Union and Mercedes had both produced racing cars thought to be unbeatable. These beasts of cars were nicknamed

'Silver Arrows' as they were unpainted and let their bare metal shine as they roared past. They were incredibly powerful and fast.

Up against eight of these formidable cars at the German GP was an old Alfa Romeo P3. It only had two-thirds of the power of the Silver Arrows, but it did have one secret weapon… Nuvolari!

He drove on the absolute limit, using all his skill and focus to maintain a ferocious race pace in his Alfa. In the end, he won by an incredible margin of 2 minutes, 14 seconds. Absolute legend! His victory shocked the German race organisers. They had been so confident of a home win that they didn't have the Italian national anthem ready to play on the podium.

BLOWOUT!

In 2024 at the Austrian Grand Prix and with fewer than 10 laps to go, Max Verstappen and Lando Norris were battling for the lead. More than 15 seconds back, George Russell was in third and thinking of settling for a podium place.

Verstappen had qualified in pole position and had commanded the race for the first 50 of the race's 71 laps. A slow pit stop, however, had cut his lead and Norris was now looming in his rear view mirror.

Norris launched attack after attack, but Verstappen held him off. It was thrilling racing, just the type of high-octane action that most race fans crave. At one point, Norris overtook Verstappen but did so while he was off the track so had to give the lead back to his rival.

On lap 64, it happened. As Norris attempted to

overtake again, the cars came together and both suffered tyre blow-outs. They carried on racing but, with punctures, their cars had far less race pace.

Russell couldn't believe his luck. He sped past both Verstappen and Norris on the way to taking the second grand prix win of his career.

GEORGE WILLIAM RUSSELL	
Born	1998, King's Lynn, England
F1 career	2019–
Total races	129
F1 wins	3

IMPOSTER!

Hans Heyer was desperate to race in Formula 1. The German was a talented driver who had won karting competitions in the 1960s and the 1974 European Touring Car Championship in a Ford Escort. However, he had very little experience of driving ultra-fast single-seater racing cars and wasn't part of an established race team.

He managed to get access to a Penske Formula 1 car and attempted to qualify for the 1977 German Grand Prix. The top 24 times in qualifying would get to take part in the race. Heyer's time around the Hockenheim track of 1 minute 57.58 seconds was decent, but only placed him twenty-seventh.

Heyer was made third reserve driver, in case three other racers pulled out before the race began. That didn't happen, but he still managed to convince officials he knew from other motorsports events, to place him and his car in the pit lane.

Moments after the race began, there was a big collision at the first corner between Clay Regazzoni and Alan Jones. During all the confusion, Heyer took his chance and drove out of the pit lane and onto the track. Outrageous!

Heyer raced for nine laps of the grand prix until his car's gearbox failed and he had to retire. It was only then that officials discovered the race had contained an imposter. Heyer received a five-race ban but it didn't matter – he had raced, albeit for a short time, in a grand prix. He is also the only driver to receive DNQ (did not qualify), DNF (did not finish) and disqualified (DSQ), all in the same race!

FANGIO STRIKES AGAIN

Juan Manuel Fangio had dominated Formula 1 in the mid-1950s, but the 1957 German Grand Prix was proving a bit of a disaster. Qualifying in fourth, he dropped a place on the opening lap before he had even reached the first corner.

Battling to get to the front in his Maserati 250F, he then suffered a terrible pit stop. One of his mechanics dropped a wheel nut which rolled underneath the car. It took half a minute to find it!

Fangio had entered the pits in first place, 30 seconds ahead of his rivals. By the time he left the pits, he was almost a minute behind them. And there were only 10 laps to go.

Fangio then produced one of the drives of his life. He broke the Nürburgring lap record seven times in a row as he forced his Maserati to ever faster and faster speeds. Amazingly, he did this while sitting on a seat that was loose and throwing him around his cockpit.

On the last-but-one lap, Fangio swooped past Mike Hawthorn to take the lead. From an impossible position, Fangio had won again. 'I have never driven that quickly before in my life and I don't think I will ever be able to do it again,' he said afterwards.

It is still rated as one of the greatest ever drives in grand prix history.

DRAG RACING

In 2011, F1 drivers got an exciting extra button in their car cockpit. It activated something called the Drag Reduction System, or DRS for short.

DRS is a flap on the rear wing of an F1 car. When the button is pushed and the flap opens, the force of drag on the car (which slows the car down) is reduced. As a result, the car can go up to 10–12 km/h faster than usual – perfect for overtaking!

DRS was designed to help drivers get past slower cars in front of them. It only works, though, if the car behind is within one second of the car in front. And it only works on parts of the track called DRS Zones. These are usually the long, straight sections of the circuit. Some tracks have just the one DRS Zone (boo!), whilst Albert Park in Australia has four (yay!).

DRS is designed to encourage more overtaking during a race, but some drivers and fans think that it's cut the fun out when a determined driver defends their position from cars behind. It is scheduled to be replaced in 2026 by a far more complicated system as F1 continues experimenting with technology to make races more action packed.

STIRLING SPORTSMANSHIP

Stirling Moss was Britain's most famous racing driver in the 1950s and 1960s. A brilliant driver of all sorts of racing cars, he is considered to be one of the best-ever F1 racers not to win the World Championship.

For four seasons in a row (1955–58), Moss came oh so close. He finished second to the legend that was Juan Fangio in 1955, 1956 and 1957. In 1956, he lost out on the World Championship by just three points.

In 1958, Moss came even closer. He had won two of the first three races and then triumphed at the Portuguese Grand Prix. In that race, his main rival for the title, Mike Hawthorn, had spun on the last lap onto the pavement and had to restart his car facing the wrong way. This was thought to be against the rules. So, Hawthorn was disqualified and lost his second-place finish, and with it six points towards the

World Championship.

In an incredible act of fair play, Moss argued with officials to let Hawthorn keep his points. He explained how Hawthorn's car had been off the track when he restarted it, which was not against the rules.

Moss's passionate defence worked. Hawthorn was reinstated in second place and kept his six points. Come the end of the season, he pipped the sporting Stirling Moss to the title by just one point.

GOING BACKWARDS

A Formula 1 Grand Prix is *usually* a marvel of organisation. Sometimes, though, things don't go as planned.

At the 1982 US Grand Prix West in Long Beach, California, the cars were completing their formation lap before taking their positions on the starting grid.

Elio de Angelis, driving a Lotus, suddenly realised he was on the wrong side of the track and in the wrong position on the starting grid. Fearing a penalty if he didn't do something about it, de Angelis started reversing his car...

...and backed straight into his teammate, Nigel Mansell, right behind.

Mansell was NOT pleased and shifted his own Lotus

into reverse. He didn't want de Angelis's car to start climbing all over his.

At that exact moment, the start lights went out and the race began. De Angelis, who had stopped reversing, sped off but Mansell was still in reverse gear. He is the only known F1 driver to start a grand prix going backwards!

LET HIM RACE

The Spanish racer, Carlos Sainz Jr had a miserable start to the 2019 Brazilian Grand Prix. His McLaren car had an engine issue, so he was unable to set a time in qualifying. He was lucky that the stewards let him enter the race, but he had to start last.

Sainz had already raced precisely 100 grand prix for Toro Rosso, Renault and McLaren, and had yet to climb the podium to celebrate a top three finish. It was unlikely that was going to change in this race, but unlikely things can happen, especially at an often eventful track like the Interlagos circuit.

Retirements, spins, overtaking moves and pit-stop strategies saw positions change frequently throughout the race. Quietly, stealthily, Sainz was moving up the field and finished the race in fourth place, just 8.9 seconds behind race winner, Max Verstappen. It was an excellent drive considering where he'd started from, but Sainz was still disappointed. He so wanted a podium.

Hours later, stewards gave Lewis Hamilton a five-second penalty. This moved him down the positions from third to seventh place and moved Sainz up to third. He'd done it! He'd finally broken his podium duck. McLaren rejoiced as it was their first podium finish for 2,072 days, since the 2014 Australian Grand Prix. It saw Sainz beat Martin Brundle's record for the most races before finishing in the top three. Since then, Sainz has won four grand prix and achieved 23 other podium finishes.

CARLOS SAINZ VÁZQUEZ DE CASTRO	
Born	1994, Madrid, Spain
F1 career	2015–
Total races	212
F1 wins	4

FIRST LAP WIPEOUT

Race officials and fans were relieved when the 1973 British Grand Prix got off to a clean start. But it didn't last long.

At the end of the first of 67 laps, Jody Scheckter's McLaren-Ford spun as it entered Woodcote Corner, bounced off the pit wall and flew back across the track. The car caused total mayhem.

'Cars were crashing all around me and I just put my head down,' recalled Scheckter afterwards. 'Then it went quiet, so I looked up – and they were still crashing, so I put my head down again.'

Scheckter's mishap had taken out eight other cars. Only one driver suffered injury: Andrea de Adamich had to retire with a broken ankle, not just from the race but from Formula 1 forever.

Amongst the wreckage were all three cars of the Surtees team. When Scheckter returned to his team in the pits, he was told to go and hide in a motorhome to avoid the Surtees team who were furious with him.

The race was restarted with 11 fewer cars than at the start. Fortunately, there was no repeat pile-up, and Peter Revson went on to win his first grand prix, with Ronnie Peterson second and Denny Hulme third.

STICK TO SLICKS

Michael Schumacher's wet weather racing skills were at their peak at the 1995 Belgian Grand Prix. Rain had ruined his chances in qualifying and the German found himself starting the race in sixteenth place – the worst starting position of his career.

While Johnny Herbert, Jean Alesi and David Coulthard battled it out at the front of the grid, Schumacher started carving it up at the rear. After just two laps, he had moved from sixteenth into the top ten and continued to progress.

Rain had fallen and the track was slippery and treacherous, but Schumacher stayed out on dry tyres, known as slicks for their lack of tread. As more and more cars headed into the pits to change onto wet tyres, Schumacher moved up the field.

Heading into the lead, still on dry tyres on a wet track, fans marvelled as he defended attack after attack by Damon Hill. Schumacher made some very aggressive moves to keep Hill from overtaking him – one of which would land him a suspended one-race ban for going too far and pushing Hill off the track.

Schumacher did eventually head into the pits for wet tyres, but the hard work had been done. He cruised to victory, more than 19 seconds ahead of Hill in second place. It was one of nine wins that season for the German, which saw him also win his second World Championship.

SIX-WHEELED WONDER

During the 1976 season, some grand prix racegoers had to rub their eyes. They couldn't believe what they were seeing. There were two Formula 1 cars on the track racing on six wheels not four.

Introduced by the Tyrrell race team, the P34 car had four 25cm-wide wheels on the front and two bigger wheels at the rear. The extra front wheels were designed to increase grip when going around a corner.

The car proved great on racetracks with long straights and corners, but not so good on bumpy, tight circuits like Brands Hatch and Monaco.

The P34's peak came at the 1976 Swedish Grand Prix, when South African driver Jody Scheckter drove the car to a memorable first place. Scheckter's teammate, Patrick Depailler from France, wasn't far behind, giving Tyrrell a one-two on the podium. Marvellous!

Although it didn't win another F1 race, the Tyrrell P34 would notch up another 12 podium places over the 1976 and 1977 seasons. It remains the only six-wheeler to have scored points in F1.

SAFETY ON TRACK

Bernd Mayländer is one of the unsung heroes of Formula 1. He's on duty at every single grand prix – yet most F1 fans don't know his name.

Mayländer is a German sports car and touring car race driver. He has been the driver of the F1 Safety Car since his debut at the 2000 Australian Grand Prix.

His current safety car is a souped-up Aston Martin Vantage. The vehicle is equipped with two radios and screens to keep him updated with race information. When he is on the track, he has to guide the racing cars round at a controlled speed, until he leaves the track when the real racing can begin again.

Called into action many times, Mayländer has led more than 700 laps of grand prix racing. But his favourite race weekends are when he isn't called into action. As he said in a 2024 interview, 'For me, the best races are those without a safety car, because that means nothing dangerous has happened on the track.'

HAWKEYE IN THE HARBOUR

Paul 'Hawkeye' Hawkins was an Australian racing driver. He came to England to work as a mechanic but also to compete in sports car competitions and other races. He won Formula Two races but only got to take part in three grand prix.

At the 1965 South African Grand Prix, he finished ninth – but it was in the next race at Monaco where he made an impact on race fans' memories, and not for the right reasons.

Hawkins was driving his Lotus-Climax car around Monaco's twisting and turning track. He was on lap 79 out of 100 when he misjudged a pair of bends called a chicane.

His Lotus spun out of control, struck some hay bales and left the track. The car flew through the air and landed in the waters of Monaco harbour! Hawkins reacted quickly and was able to free himself from his sinking car and swim to safety.

His car was retrieved from the harbour and fitted with a lifebuoy painted with his brand new nickname, the 'Swimming Kangaroo'. Alberto Ascari had been the first driver to crash into Monaco harbour in 1955, but Hawkins was the last... so far.

ROBERT PAUL HAWKINS	
Born	1937, Richmond, Australia
F1 career	1965
Total races	3
F1 wins	0

THE TEA TRAY

March entered Formula 1 racing in 1970 with a regular racing car but their car for the 1971 season, the March 711, was radical. It certainly turned heads and raised eyebrows.

It was a completely new design with big side pods that channelled air into the engine radiators. Upfront, it had a surprisingly large, rounded nose, while mounted on top was a giant, oval-shaped aerofoil that looked like the wing of a Spitfire fighter plane from World War II. No one in F1 had seen anything like it.

The aerofoil was designed to direct air that flowed past. This helped increase downforce, the force that pushes cars down onto the track. Greater downforce increases tyre grip on the track, which proved vital especially when taking tight turns and corners.

Quickly nicknamed 'the tea tray' and initially mocked, the March 711 turned out to be no laughing matter. In the hands of Swedish driver, Ronnie Peterson, March finished second in four races including the 1971 Monaco Grand Prix. These results saw the newish team finish a creditable fourth in the Constructors' Championship, while Peterson came second in the Drivers' Championship behind Jackie Stewart.

March are remembered for giving a debut that season to a young Austrian driver who would win three World Championships: Niki Lauda. But more immediately, more teams started to pay more attention to aerodynamics, researching and testing ways of using wings to boost their cars' performance.

CLIVE GIFFORD

PROST V SENNA

Race fans in the 1980s were treated to one of the greatest of all F1 rivalries. It reached a peak in 1988 and 1989 when the pair were in the same McLaren team.

In the blue-helmeted corner was Alain Prost. This French driver was cool and calculating. He was a great tactician and a master at looking after his car's brakes, engine and fuel throughout a race, so that he was still challenging at the end.

In the yellow and green-helmeted corner was Ayrton Senna. This Brazilian driver was frighteningly quick, aggressive and drove spectacularly. Sometimes, this resulted in bumps and shunts with rival race cars, especially with Prost.

During those two years at McLaren, Senna won more

races (14–11) but Prost gained more podium finishes (25–18) and championship points (163–150). Both won a championship, but they clashed with each other on and off the track.

Things came to a head at both the 1989 and 1990 end-of-season races at Japan's Suzuka circuit. In both races, they crashed into each other, as one tried to pass and the other would not yield. Each alleged dirty tricks by the other – yet after Prost had retired in 1993, and towards the end of Senna's life, the two struck up a friendship and rang each other every week to discuss life and Formula 1. It turned out that these two contrasting drivers weren't quite so different after all.

AYRTON SENNA DA SILVA	
Born	1960, Santana, Brazil
F1 career	1984–94
Total races	162
F1 wins	41

CLIVE GIFFORD

DIAMONDS AREN'T FOREVER

Sometimes, F1 teams join forces with sponsors to promote a particular event or product. Consequently, cars can be decorated in some pretty peculiar ways.

In 2004, the Jaguar Racing team partnered up with the movie, *Ocean's Twelve*, all about a jewel heist. Jaguar fitted a real diamond, worth £150,000, to the nose of each of its two racing cars.

When the race began, it soon became obvious what a silly idea this was. Jaguar driver Christian Klien crashed into the Loews Barrier of the Monaco track and was out of the race. In all the kerfuffle and confusion of getting the wrecked car off the track, no one could find the diamond.

The Jaguar team and race officials searched and searched and searched. No luck. Had the diamond been smashed in the crash? Unlikely, as it's the hardest natural substance on Earth. Had it simply been lost or had someone stolen it?

To this day, the diamond has never been recovered. The story of the missing diamond, though, did drum up huge amounts of publicity for the *Ocean's Twelve* movie.

CHAOS IN CANADA

The 1973 Canadian Grand Prix was meant to be a landmark in F1 organisation: it was the first grand prix to feature a safety car. This vehicle was designed to lead the racing cars around the track after there had been an accident or some other problem. The cars had to stay in their order, and they couldn't overtake while behind the safety car.

Filthy, wet conditions on the track in Canada saw a number of mistakes made by drivers. Some cars ended up spinning while, on the thirty-second lap, two collided. So out came F1's first safety car – a Porsche 914 driven by racing driver, Eppie Wietzes.

Wietzes guided the Porsche in front of the Williams car driven by the New Zealander, Howden Ganley, assuming he was the race leader. But other cars were farther round the track and joined the back of the cars behind the safety car. This was in an era before there was electronic timing of all cars, so it was much harder to keep a 100 per cent accurate record.

The race eventually continued and many laps later, Ganley celebrated after crossing the line seemingly first. But other teams thought one of their drivers were a lap ahead of Ganley; Britain's Jackie Oliver, Emerson Fittipaldi from Brazil and the USA's Peter Revson all thought they had won the race.

Hours of heated discussions were held after the race, the outcome of which led to the demotion of poor Howden Ganley, from first to sixth. The winner turned out to be Peter Revson, with Fittipaldi second and Oliver third.

SUPER COOPER

The Cooper-Climax T51 was a racing car designed in 1958–59 by Owen Maddock and built in Surrey, England. At the time, most F1 cars had their engines mounted in front of the driver. But Maddock had placed the T51's engine, built by Climax, just behind the cockpit. We now call this a mid-mounted engine. The car was lighter than many of its rivals and sleek. It was a radical design for 1959, but would it be any good?

Australian driver Jack Brabham (see p. 24) took to his T51 immediately. He won two races, finished second or third three times, and became World Champion. Immediately, demand for the car soared and the Cooper Car Company were happy to help.

Twenty-five cars lined up on the starting grid for the 1960 British Grand Prix. A record nine of the vehicles were Cooper-Climax T51s. Four further cars on the grid were Coopers but fitted with other makes of engine. It was no surprise when a T51 won the race, driven by Brabham who was on the way to his second World Championship in a row.

WHAT A COMEBACK

'I would rather drive a truck than this car.' – Alain Prost.

It's not exactly glowing praise for a new race vehicle, is it? Especially, one that a race team had spent millions on. Alain Prost was nicknamed 'The Professor' for his cool, calculating brain and racing style. So, when he criticised his new Ferrari car, the 643, during the 1991 F1 season, people took notice.

His employers didn't like it. They sensationally sacked him later that season, with the Australian Grand Prix still to be raced. The F1 paddock was amazed. Ferrari had fired a three-time world champion.

Prost sat out the 1992 season and race fans wondered whether he would return to the sport. Secretly, he was already negotiating with Frank Williams to join his team. Prost was always good with the techy side of racing and understood that Williams were likely to have the best car the next season.

Prost and Williams proved a perfect match. He won 7 of the 16 races in the 1993 season as well as coming second three times and third twice. He also grabbed pole position in 13 of the races – an astonishing feat.

This resulted in Prost winning his fourth World Championship to go with those in 1985, 1986 and 1989. With the 1993 season over, he retired again, this time for good.

ALAIN PROST	
Born	1955, Lorette, France
F1 career	1980–91, 1993
Total races	202
F1 wins	51

KNIGHT RIDER

Jack Brabham was already a two-time F1 World Champion (1959, 1960) when he started his own race team with engineer Ron Tauranac. Brabham thought he could develop and build his own car which could compete with big teams like Ferrari and Lotus.

In 1966, Brabham powered his BT19 racing car with an engine from Australian company, Repco. The engine wasn't the most powerful, but it was light and compact. It proved to be pretty reliable in race conditions as well.

That season, Brabham won four grand prix in his own car. Coupled with a second and a fourth place finish, the Australian won the championship for the third time. He remains the only driver to win a World Championship driving his own car.

The Brabham company were flooded with orders to build vehicles for other race teams and competitions outside of Formula 1. By 1970, they'd built more than 500 single-seater racing cars.

Brabham's team won three more World Championships in 1968 with Denny Hulme (while Brabham finished second), and in 1981 and 1983 with Nelson Piquet driving. In 1979, he became the first racing driver to be knighted by Queen Elizabeth II.

CLIVE GIFFORD

THE SINGAPORE SLING

What do Maggotts, Eau Rouge and the Swimming Pool all have in common?

They're all the names of famous turns on tracks which host grand prix races. These corners – either smooth and flowing or tight and technical – are scenic and much-loved features of race circuits. Maggotts is part of Silverstone, and Eau Rouge is found at Spa, while the Swimming Pool is an iconic feature of Monaco's Monte Carlo circuit.

A much-less loved corner arrived in 2008 at the Marina Bay Circuit, home to the Singapore Grand Prix. Named the Singapore Sling, it was actually three turns in one: a quick left, then a narrow right and finally, another narrow left, each fitted with sausage-shaped kerbs.

F1 drivers were unimpressed when the Sling was unveiled and then, things got worse. It was tough to drive at speed and many drivers hit a kerb, went airborne and crashed into one of the track barriers. Victims of the Sling included Kimi Räikkönen, Giancarlo Fisichella, Adrian Sutil and Kamui Kobayashi.

'It's the worst corner I've ever driven in Formula 1,' was Lewis Hamilton's zero-star review.

Come the 2013 Singapore Grand Prix and the Sling had gone. It had been replaced by a single flowing corner at turn 10 of the track. It made the circuit a little faster and the drivers a lot happier.

FATHER AND SON

Michael and Mick Schumacher, Gilles and Jacques Villeneuve, Keke and Nico Rosberg, are just a few of the fathers and sons who have both raced in Formula 1. 2024 champion Max Verstappen's dad, Jos, raced 107 times for seven different F1 teams.

But for success across the generations, you cannot beat Graham and Damon Hill.

Graham Hill didn't get his driving licence until he was 24 years old. He made up for lost time by becoming a racing all-rounder. He remains the only driver to win the big three competitions of world motorsport, the F1 World Championship, the Indy 500 race in America and the Le Mans 24 Hours endurance race.

Twenty-nine years after his father won the second of his two World Championships, Damon Hill was taking part in the 1996 Japanese Grand Prix. He just needed to score a point to secure the title but did much better that that. He won the race, his eighth victory of the season, making the Hills the only father and son duo to both win the F1 World Championship.

NORMAN GRAHAM HILL	
Born	1929, London, England
F1 career	1958–75
Total races	179
F1 wins	14

THREE WHEELS, SIX POINTS

The 1987 German Grand Prix was absolute carnage for the cars that took part. Twenty-six vehicles lined up on the starting grid, but the Hockenheim circuit took its toll.

Riccardo Patrese was first to retire, on lap 5, with an ignition problem, followed by René Arnoux, Ivan Capelli and Satoru Nakajima. By lap 23, half the field were out of the race.

They were quickly followed by Nigel Mansell with engine failure on lap 25 and Alain Prost with electrical problems.

Only six cars were left, and it could have been only five: just as he started his last lap, Stefan Johansson was battling with his McLaren MP4/3. His car's tyres were losing grip on the tricky circuit.

BANG!

His front right tyre suffered a puncture. Within seconds, the tyre was wrecked and shredded, leaving the metal wheel exposed. The suspension arm broke, too. So, incredibly carefully, Johansson had to guide his damaged vehicle round the rest of the lap on three wheels. He crossed the line in his three-wheeler to finish second, ahead of Ayrton Senna. What a finish!

CLIVE GIFFORD

ACADEMY ABBI

The F1 Academy for talented young women racers had a new star in 2024. After a quiet 2023 season, Abbi Pulling from Lincolnshire shredded the opposition.

Racing for the Rodin Motorsport team, Pulling was disappointed with the first race of the season in Jeddah, Saudi Arabia. Try as she might, she just couldn't beat French driver, Doriane Pin. After that, though, Pulling's results were simply SENSATIONAL!

Pulling's finishes in the fifteen-race 2024 F1 Academy season															
Race	1	2	3	4	5	6	7	8	9	10	11	12	13	14	15
Position	2nd	1st	1st	1st	1st	2nd	1st	3rd	1st	1st	2nd	X	1st	1st	2nd
X = race cancelled															

In November 2024, Pulling celebrated winning the championship with races to spare after winning in Qatar. Or so she thought. The organisers later added another race to the next race weekend which meant her lead of 83 points over Pin could still be overtaken.

Like a true champion, Pulling shelved any disappointment and regained her focus. At the next race weekend in Abu Dhabi, she rocketed round the track to gain pole position and the crucial points she needed, which meant she could no longer be beaten.

Pulling celebrated being champion (again) by winning two of the three races of the weekend. It was a truly dominant season for the 21-year-old speed demon.

PASS CLASS

The world of Formula 1 is braced for a big set of rule changes in 2026. The fuel the cars use to race will be sustainable and the cars themselves lighter, narrower and more agile. The aim is to increase the chances of overtaking. Fans love it when one car passes by another during a race.

There have been contests, like the 2009 European Grand Prix and the 2021 Belgian Grand Prix, where there wasn't a single overtaking move in the entire race. Boring!

But there have also been epic races like the 2016 Chinese Grand Prix which were a festival of overtaking. Nico Rosberg in his Mercedes won the race, but there were so many changes of position, it was hard for commentators and spectators to keep up.

Kimi Räikkönen, Lewis Hamilton and Sebastian Vettel all found themselves in lowly positions during the race and responded by passing plenty of other cars. The grand total of overtakes in the race was a stunning 161. It helped that despite bumps and shunts, all 22 starters finished the race – a pretty rare event.

Formula 1 will continue to tinker with its rules to try to get the most out of its amazing tech and brilliant drivers.

CLIVE GIFFORD

SUPER MARIO

Mario Andretti was 15 years old when his family moved from Italy to settle in the United States. Before he emigrated, he had been in the crowd for the 1954 Italian GP at Monza and loved it, soon becoming hooked on racing. Once in the US, he threw himself into racing in all sorts of competitions and became an incredibly versatile driver. He won NASCAR races like the Daytona 500, endurance races and four IndyCar championships. But could he also do it in Formula 1?

He entered F1 part-time between 1968 and 1972 and even turned down an offer from Ferrari to be their number-one driver. He had lots of sponsorship and offers to drive back in North America which he couldn't turn his back on.

Later in the 1970s, Andretti came back to F1, first with the American Parnelli team and then with Lotus. In

1978, the combination of Andretti and the Lotus 79 car were a real force. Andretti's pace in qualifying was devastating and he began half of the 16 races on pole position.

Six race wins meant that Mario Andretti was crowned World Champion after the Italian Grand Prix, still with two races of the 1978 season to go. He was America's last F1 champion.

In 2026, a new American race team will be joining Formula 1, Cadillac F1. Mario has been made a director of the team. 'My first love was Formula 1 and now – 70 years later – the F1 paddock is still my happy place,' he said on the day of the announcement.

MARIO GABRIELE ANDRETTI	
Born	1940, Montona, Italy
F1 career	1968–72, 1974–82
Total races	131
F1 wins	12